Engaging the Families and Immigrants

Learn how to engage the diverse families of English learners (ELs) and immigrants with the effective, practical approaches in this book. This must-have resource for teachers and school leaders is packed with fresh ideas geared toward building a partnership between school communities and ELs and immigrant families at school and at home. The book includes information and activities to:

◆ Assess current practices
◆ Investigate family perceptions and expectations
◆ Overcome challenges
◆ Improve communication
◆ Fund family engagement

Fully revised and up-to-date, the new edition shines a much-needed spotlight on immigrant families from numerous homelands and includes a chapter on schools and organizations that have applied many of the ideas in the book for successful partnerships. New online resources include 20 new activities to complement the book chapters, over 50 annotated websites, and additional book recommendations to provide insight into the immigrant experience. The support materials can be found at routledge.com/9780367607548.

Organized with the busy educator in mind, this book can be read straight through or section by section to best fit your specific needs.

As the demographics of America's schools continue to grow and change, this book guides you to building an inclusive school community in which every family can thrive!

Renee Rubin is an educational consultant specializing in literacy, ELs, and family engagement. Previously, she taught in elementary schools for 11 years and taught pre-service and in-service teachers at the University of Texas at Brownsville for 13 years.

Michelle H. Abrego is an Assistant Professor in the Organization and School Leadership Department in the College of Education and P-16 Integration at the University of Texas Rio Grande Valley, USA.

John A. Sutterby is an Associate Professor in the Department of Interdisciplinary Learning and Teaching at the University of Texas at San Antonio, USA.

Eye on Education

Enlivening Instruction with Drama and Improv:
A Guide for Second Language and World Language Teachers
Melisa Cahnmann-Taylor and Kathleen R. McGovern

Leading Your World Language Program:
Strategies for Design and Supervision, Even If You Don't
Speak the Language!
Catherine Ritz

The Classroom Teacher's Guide to Supporting English Language Learners
Pamela Mesta and Olga Reber

Differentiated Instruction:
A Guide for World Language Teachers, 2nd Edition
Deborah Blaz

The World Language Teacher's Guide to Active Learning:
Strategies and Activities for Increasing Student Engagement, 2nd Edition
Deborah Blaz

An Educator's Guide to Dual Language Instruction:
Increasing Achievement and Global Competence, K-12
Gayle Westerberg and Leslie Davison

Determining Difference from Disability:
What Culturally Responsive Teachers Should Know
Gerry McCain and Megan Farsnworth

Powerful Parent Partnerships:
Rethinking Family Engagement for Student Success
Robert Dillon and Melisa Nixon

What Great Principals Do Differently:
Twenty Things that Matter Most, 3rd Edition
Todd Whitaker

What Great Teachers Do Differently:
Nineteen Things That Matter Most, 3rd Edition
Todd Whitaker

Teaching Practices from America's Best Urban Schools:
A Guide for School and Classroom Leaders, 2nd Edition
Joseph F. Johnson, Jr., Cynthia L. Uline and Lynne G. Perez

Engaging the Families of ELs and Immigrants

Ideas, Resources, and Activities

Renee Rubin, Michelle H. Abrego, John A. Sutterby

2nd Edition

Routledge
Taylor & Francis Group

NEW YORK AND LONDON

Second edition published 2021
by Routledge
605 Third Avenue, New York, NY 10158

and by Routledge
2 Park Square, Milton Park, Abingdon, Oxon, OX14 4RN

Routledge is an imprint of the Taylor & Francis Group, an informa business

First edition published by Eye on Education 2012

Library of Congress Cataloging-in-Publication Data
Names: Rubin, Renee, 1954– author. | Abrego, Michelle H, author. |
Sutterby, John A., author.
Title: Engaging the families of ELS and immigrants: ideas, resources, and
activities / Renee Rubin, Michelle H. Abrego, John A. Sutterby.
Description: [2nd ed.] | New York: Routledge, 2021.
Identifiers: LCCN 2021009874 (print) | LCCN 2021009875 (ebook) |
ISBN 9780367609399 (hardback) | ISBN 9780367607548 (paperback) |
ISBN 9781003102601 (ebook)
Subjects: LCSH: English language—Study and teaching—Foreign speakers. |
Education—Parent participation—United States. |
English language—United States. | Language and languages—United States.
Classification: LCC PE1128.A2 R83 2021 (print) | LCC PE1128.A2 (ebook) |
DDC 428.0071—dc23
LC record available at https://lccn.loc.gov/2021009874
LC ebook record available at https://lccn.loc.gov/2021009875

ISBN: 9780367609399 (hbk)
ISBN: 9780367607548 (pbk)
ISBN: 9781003102601 (ebk)

Typeset in Palatino
by codeMantra

Access the Support Material: www.routledge.com/9780367607548

Contents

List of Illustrations xi
Meet the Authors xii
Preface xiii
Acknowledgments xv
Notes on the Support Material xvi

1 Partnering for Student Success **1**
Scenario: Arriving from Mexico 1
New Immigrants in U.S. Schools 2
Changing Demographics of America's Schools 3
    Immigrant Families 3
    Languages 3
Benefits of Family Partnerships 3
    Student Benefits 4
    Family Benefits 4
    Teacher Benefits 4
    Schoolwide Benefits 5
Challenges to Family Engagement 5
    Differing Expectations 5
    Language Barriers 6
    Lack of Educator Preparation 6
    Digital Divide 6
Educator Professional Development 6
    Self-Awareness 7
    Awareness of Immigrant Families 7
    Communication 9
    Respect 9
Activity: Attitudes about Family Engagement 10
Activity: Immigrant Family Panel 12
Relevant Literature 13
References 13

2 Finding Out What Families Want **16**
Scenario: Investigating What Families Want 16
Family Needs Assessments 17
Scenario: Differing Expectations 18
Surveys 19
    Satisfaction Surveys 19

Open-Ended Questions   19
Providing Background Information   20
Appropriate Survey Topics   20
Digital Survey Tools   21
Equitable Data Collection   22
Beyond Surveys   23
Focus Groups   24
Topics of Interest   25
Comprehensive Planning   25
Activity: Analyze School Needs Assessment Practices   26
Activity: Focus Groups   27
Relevant Literature   28
References   29

3 **Creating a Welcoming School Environment**   **30**
Scenario: All Families Welcome!   30
Importance of School Climate   31
What Makes a Welcoming School?   32
Immigrant Families and Orientation   33
Evaluating the School Environment   35
Welcoming Atmosphere and Language   35
Safe and Welcoming   36
Undocumented Families   37
Immigrants' Legal Rights   38
Sensitive Location   38
Discipline Policies   38
School Safety   38
Parent Spaces   39
Schools as Community Resources   39
Library   39
Nurse's Office/Health Services   40
Gyms/Sports Fields   40
Summer   40
After-School Programs   40
Building Community   41
Activity: Knowing Your School Community   41
Activity: Mystery Shopper   42
Activity: School Safety Survey   43
Relevant Literature   45
References   45

4 **Communicating with Immigrant Families**   **48**
Scenario: Summer Contact   48
Building Relationships   49
Language   50

Interpretation Law   51
Interpretation Effectiveness   51
Recruiting and Training Interpreters   53
Educators Preparing to Work with Interpreters   54
Using Graphs to Communicate   54
Culture and Expectations   55
Virtual Communication   55
Digital Availability and Knowledge   56
Telephone Communication   57
Parent–Teacher Conferences   58
Community Outreach   59
Home Visits   59
Families to Families   59
Activity: Difficult Communication Practice Scenarios   60
Activity: Evaluating School–Home Communication   62
Activity: Telephone Communication   63
Relevant Literature   63
References   64

5 **Learning at Home**   **66**
Scenario: Immigrants Teaching at Home   66
Emphasize the Positive   67
All Families Can Help Their Children Learn   67
Asking Families   68
Home Learning without the Internet   68
Scenario: School Bus Hotspot   69
Online Learning   69
Digital Challenges   69
Resources in Languages Other Than English   70
Hybrid Learning   71
Scenario: Challenges Faced at Home   71
Traditional Homework   72
Connect Families with Community Help   73
Activity: Family Interviews   74
Activity: Grocery Store Math   75
Activity: Nutrition and Health   75
Activity: Online Read-Alouds   76
Activity: Technology for Families   77
Activity: Vocabulary Expansion from Home   78
Relevant Literature   79
References   79

6 **Beyond Open Houses**   **81**
Scenario: Positive Meeting   81
What Families Want   82

Language 83
Different Types of Events 83
    Helping Immigrant Families Understand U.S. Schools 84
    Breaking Down Stereotypes 84
    Online Workshops 85
    Community Partnerships 86
    Family Leadership Preparation 87
Activity: Job Fair 88
Activities: Leadership and Advocacy Preparation 88
Activity: Missing Pieces of the Curriculum 90
Activity: Standardized Testing 92
Activity: Virtual Science Workshop 93
Relevant Literature 93
References 94

7 **Partnering with Families of Students with Special Needs** 96
Scenario: Active Child 96
Language and Culture 97
Families Sharing Important Information 98
Accommodations in the Inclusive Classroom 98
Assessments 100
Scenario: Assessment Difficulties 100
Individualized Education Plan (IEP) Meetings 101
    Student Involvement in IEPs 103
    On-Going Communication 103
Individualizing for Families 104
    Cultural Beliefs about Special Needs 104
    Stress from Special Needs 104
    Family Members with Special Needs 104
Gifted and Talented Programs 105
Bullying 105
Activity: Bullying Role Playing 106
Activity: Special Needs Resources 107
Relevant Literature 108
References 108

8 **Immigrant Families under Stress** 111
Scenario: New Students 111
Sources of Stress and Trauma 111
Hierarchy of Needs 112
    Food and Shelter 112
    Safety and Security 113
    Relationships and Belonging 114

Personal Discrimination 114

Structural Discrimination 114

Family Discrimination 115

Reducing Discrimination 115

Self-Esteem and Accomplishment 116

Achieving Goals 118

Angry Families 118

Scenario: Failing Test Scores 118

Activity: Community Resources 120

Activity: Questioning Prejudices 121

Activity: Talking to Children about Diversity 122

Relevant Literature 122

References 123

9 Funding Family Engagement **126**

Scenario: Reality Hits 126

Introduction 127

Federal Monies under Every Student Succeeds Act 128

Title I Federal Funds 129

Title III Federal Funds 129

Title II and IV Federal Funds 130

Partnerships 130

Organizations that Support Immigrants 130

Adult ESL Programs 131

Other Community Partnerships 131

Parent Teacher Associations/Organizations 131

Service and Faith Based Organizations 132

Blessings in a Backpack 132

Recruiting Volunteers 133

Retired Volunteers 133

High School Volunteers 133

College and University Volunteers 134

Volunteer Initiatives 134

Grant Writing 135

Online Grant Search Tools 135

National PTA Grants 135

Gardening Grants 135

Fundraising Events 136

Restaurant Spirit Nights 136

Drive-a-Thons 136

Crowdfunding 137

Conclusion 137

Activity: Family Engagement Funding Team 138

Activity: Making Connections 138

Relevant Literature   139
References   140

10 Success Stories   **142**
Introduction   142
School Success Stories   142
   Klein Independent School District (ISD)   142
   Rogers Public Schools, Arkansas   145
   Shelby County Schools   146
   Washoe County Schools   147
Family Leadership Initiative Success Stories   149
   Padres Comprometidos   149
   Parent Institute for Quality Education   150
   Portland Empowered   152
   OneAmerica   153
Partnerships with Other Community Based Organizations   154
   Aim High   154
   SkyART   155
   STEM (Science, Technology, Engineering, and Mathematics)   156
Success Stories Key Take-Aways   158
Activity: Reflection on Successful Practices   159
Relevant Literature   159
Success Stories Websites   160
References   160

Illustrations

Figures

4.1 Spectrum of Interpretation Options (Gardner, 2020b)   51
10.1 Klein Independent School District Strategic Plan   143
10.2 Dual Capacity Building Framework (Mapp and Bergman, 2019)   144

Tables

1.1 ELLs, ELs, and Emergent Bilinguals   3
3.1 Possible Orientation Topics   34
3.2 Various Immigrant Statuses   37
4.1 Interpretation and Translation   50
6.1 Guidelines for Successful Events   83
6.2 Different Types of School Language Programs   85
7.1 Accommodations and Modifications   99
7.2 Pre-IEP Meeting Checklist for Families   102
8.1 Racism, Prejudice, and Discrimination as Used in This Book   114
8.2 Ways to Reduce Discrimination   115
8.3 Dealing with Angry Families   119
9.1 Sample Template for Family Engagement Plan   128

Meet the Authors

Renee Rubin is an educational consultant, specializing in family engagement, emergent bilinguals, and literacy. She currently lives in New Jersey, but she has taught elementary school through graduate school in New Mexico and Texas. With the other authors, she designed and implemented an after-school program at a local elementary school in which undergraduate and graduate students interacted weekly with emergent bilinguals and their families. She also served as Co-Principal Investigator for a U.S. Department of Education Early Childhood Educator Professional Development Grant.

Michelle H. Abrego is currently an assistant professor in the Organization and School Leadership Department in the College of Education and P-16 Integration with the University of Texas Rio Grande Valley. She is a former teacher, principal, program director at the Texas Education Agency, educational consultant, author, and higher education faculty member. Her research interests include family engagement, school leadership preparation, and the support and development of new teachers.

John A. Sutterby is an associate professor at the University of Texas San Antonio (UTSA) in the department of Interdisciplinary Learning and Teaching. At UTSA, he teaches course in early childhood education and action research. His research interests include children's literature, children's play, and play environments and play and social justice. He has twice served as president of The Association for the Study of Play.

Preface

Engaging the Families of ELs and Immigrants: Ideas, Resources, and Activities, 2nd Ed., is a practical guide to facilitate the engagement of families of ELs and immigrants in the schools. Readers can choose the information, activities, and resources that best fit their situation. A new chapter highlights successful family engagement programs.

This book was rewritten while the pandemic raged, and most schools were closed for some months to in-person instruction. The essential role of all families in their children's education became even more apparent. The pandemic also shone a light on the challenges of online learning, which are discussed throughout the book. If students are going to catch up from the pandemic and if achievement gaps are going to be narrowed or closed, families will need to play an important role. This book provides some ideas of how schools can partner with all families now and in the future.

Families of ELs and immigrants represent a broad spectrum of cultures and experiences. Rather than making assumptions about the schools or families, the authors have provided activities that will help schools learn more about the EL and immigrant families in their community, including their strengths and their aspirations for their children.

This new edition highlights immigrant families from a wider variety of cultural and linguistic backgrounds. The relevant literature in each chapter was chosen to reflect the families' experiences and expand understanding of the students in our schools.

We have tried to use vocabulary that values immigrant families and their multiple languages as much as possible. We use "collaborating, partnering, and communicating" to indicate equal relationships rather than "involving" which suggests the school is doing something to or for the families. We use "emergent bilinguals" because we believe multiple languages are assets.

Chapter 1 provides an overview of the benefits of engaging families in the schools, some of the challenges, and ways to meet those challenges. Chapter 2 discusses ways to find out what families really want for their children and from the school. Chapter 3 suggests ways to make schools welcoming for all families. Chapter 4 examines communication with families and the use of interpretation and translation. Chapter 5 reviews different types of learning at home and the challenges of online learning. Chapter 6 has ideas and rationale for family events that go well beyond open houses. Chapter 7 discusses forming essential partnerships with families who have children with special needs. Chapter 8 examines the trauma and discrimination experienced by immigrant families and some ways to support these families. Chapter 9 suggests ways of funding and finding volunteers to assist with family engagement. Chapter 10 highlights successful school districts, family initiatives, and other community organizations that support EL and immigrant families in their efforts to participate in their children's education. New to this edition are supplemental online activities and resources, available on the Routledge website.

This book tries to respond to the growing number of immigrant families. One out of every four children in the United States now has at least one immigrant parent. Although the book focuses on EL and immigrant families in the United States, most of the ideas, activities, and resources can be applied to all families. Engaging families is more important now than ever for student success.

Acknowledgments

We would like to thank the following individuals for their contributions.

Ali, Pious: Staff, Portland Empowered

Amargós, Carlos: Outreach and Engagement Specialist, Rogers Public Schools

Arbuckle, Lance: Principal, Rogers New Technology High School, Rogers Public Schools

Bulale, Nimco: Education Program Manager, One America

Chavez, Patricia E.: Director of Policy, Parent Institute for Quality Education (PIQE)

Colón, Ingrid T.: Education Research Program Manager, UnidosUS

Corral, Gloria: President & CEO, Parent Institute for Quality Education (PIQE)

Crain, D'Lisa: Family Schools Partnerships Administrator, Washoe County Schools

Gardner, Laura: Founder, Immigrant Connections

Hamid, Ayesha F.: Author, *Borderland Between Worlds: A Memoir*

Hamilton, Elizabeth Campos: Region III Director, Learning Disabilities Association, Illinois

Juárez, Cheryl: Principal Investigator, Children Investigating Science with Parents & Afterschool

Lee, Alec L.: Executive Director Aim High

Mayer, Patricia: Vice President Program Development, Parent Institute for Quality Education

Mapp, Karen: Senior Lecturer, Harvard University

Norouzi, Roxana: Deputy Director, One America

Ovalle-Lopez, Maria: Family Engagement Director, Klein Independent School District

Rodriguez, Jose: Director Parent and Community Engagement, UnidosUS

Schroeder, Claire: Staff, Portland Empowered

Scott, Zach: Senior Manager of Federal Engagement and Outreach Advocacy, National Association of Secondary Schools Principals

Shepard, Nicole: Communications Project Manager Klein Independent School District

Soler, Ana: Chairperson, National Accreditation of Educational Translators and Interpreters of Spoken Languages

Thurston, Linda P.: Co-author, *Collaboration, Consultation, and Teamwork for Students with Special Needs*

Ubaldo, Yesenia: Community Engagement Advisor, Shelby County Schools

Van Houten-Maldonado, Devon: Director of Programs, SkyART

Villalpando, Cristina: Bilingual Counselor, Shelby County Schools

Notes on the Support Material

Website links, additional activities and literature that support the content of the book are available on the Routledge website as Adobe Acrobat files. Permission has been granted to purchasers of this book to download these tools and print them. You can access these downloads by visiting https://www.routledge.com/9780367607548. Then click on the tab that says "Support Material" and select the files. They will begin downloading to your computer.

1

Partnering for Student Success

Scenario: Arriving from Mexico

In the middle of November, Sandra Martinez arrived in Charlotte, North Carolina, from Monterrey, Mexico, with her three children—Marco, age eight; Araceli, age six; and Margot, age three. They had just gotten their visas to join her husband who was working in the United States.

She was a little surprised and unprepared for the cold rain that greeted them on their arrival. Her husband met them at the airport and drove them to the small home he had rented for their arrival. Later that day, he drove them all to the local Walmart to purchase warm clothes.

After settling in, she knew her first task would be to take the older children to school. One of her neighbors, Victoria Mendoza, was a recent immigrant from Hidalgo, Mexico. Victoria offered to go with Sandra since she spoke enough English to translate for the newcomer family.

Marco and Araceli looked immaculate in their new school uniforms that their parents purchased at Walmart. As they walked up to Sallie Smith Elementary, they were a little nervous. The secretary seemed friendly as she handed over the many forms that had to be filled in and signed. The papers seemed endless. Finally, when they were all filled in, the secretary skimmed them and announced that Marco would be joining Ms. Parker's third-grade class while Araceli would be placed in first grade. The secretary then called an office, and they were joined by a tall, well-dressed woman. She was Ms. Anderson, the assistant principal.

"Ms. Anderson will be taking the children to their new classrooms," she said.

"Can't I go with them?" Sandra asked through the interpreter. "Sorry," Ms. Anderson replied. "Our school policy is to not let parents into the classrooms." Sandra looked worried. "They'll be fine," Ms. Anderson reassured her. "Vamos, let's go," she said to the children, who rose obediently and after hugging their mother, followed the tall woman out the door. Sandra was left with many doubts and concerns, which she shared with Victoria on the way home.

"I understand," Victoria replied. "But we have to adapt to the way they do things here."

New Immigrants in U.S. Schools

It is easy to understand why schools don't want families walking into class during instruction, but it is also easy to understand the parent's point of view. The parent is new to the country, doesn't speak English, and is used to a different education system. She wants to meet the children's teachers and see where they will be spending their days. What are some other ways this situation could have been handled? It can be difficult when schools have not had much experience working with immigrants who do not speak English.

New immigrants to the United States often have difficulty understanding the school system here. They generally come with very different experiences in their home countries. It can be especially difficult if they do not speak English well. Much confusion can occur when school personnel are not prepared to work with families from differing linguistic and cultural backgrounds. Those of us who have grown up in the American school system may find the actions or decisions made by these families strange or unusual. They may be thinking the same things about us. Educators who understand this will better be able to help new immigrants make a smooth transition into school. (See more about *Creating a Welcoming School Environment* in Chapter 3.)

New immigrants like Sandra are proactive in dealing with the school system. One way they try to figure out the school system is to take advantage of local networks to help them navigate it. These may be other parents, community leaders, or religious leaders. New immigrants also seek out school personnel who speak their own language, whether they are custodians or school secretaries. The purpose of this text is to help educators better understand some ways they can help families make the transition to a U.S. school, as well as making schools a more welcoming place for new immigrants. A smooth transition for both families and school personnel can help children better succeed.

Changing Demographics of America's Schools

Immigrant Families

Schools all across the nation are experiencing influxes of immigrant students from all over the world. In 2017, one quarter of all students in the United States had at least one immigrant parent born outside the United States (Urban Institute, 2019). Although their parents were born elsewhere, 90 percent of these 18.6 million children are U.S. citizens. By 2065, The Pew Research Center predicts that one in three Americans will be immigrants or children of immigrants (Cohn, 2015). Due to the aging US population, immigrants will be needed to build the labor force and support social security.

Languages

The number of English learners in the United States grew 28.1 percent between the 2000–2001 school year and the 2016–2017 school year, totaling almost 5 million students (Office of English Language Acquisition, 2020). (See table 1.1). Spanish is the predominant home language for almost three-quarters of English learners with Arabic and Chinese next (National Center for Education Statistics, 2020). Even less common languages have grown in numbers. Over 16,000 students reported that Swahili was their home language and 14,100 students reported that Nepali was their home language. Cities ranging from New York to Wichita, Kansas, now have over 100 different languages spoken in student homes. Rogers, Arkansas, with a total population of 68,000 people has 51 languages spoken in students' homes.

Benefits of Family Partnerships

When schools, families, and communities collaborate, everyone benefits. *Family* in this book refers to anyone who is concerned and partners with the

Table 1.1 ELLs, ELs, and Emergent Bilinguals

English Language Learner (ELL) or English Learner (EL)	Emergent Bilingual
ELL and EL are terms used by the federal government to identify students who are learning to speak, read, and write English. Students usually lose this designation when they have reached a certain level of English proficiency.	Emergent bilingual indicates that someone is learning a second language while maintaining the first language. This term values bilingualism as an asset. Emergent multilingual is used for more than two languages.

school for student success. This may be parents, foster parents, sponsors, grandparents, or even neighbors or mentors. Family and community collaboration with schools has been shown to be one of the best predictors of student learning and overall development in studies for the past 50 years (Hornby & Blackwell, 2018). Recognizing this fact, The Every Student Succeeds Act (2015) mandates family engagement and earmarks funding for its implementation. The goal is to create partnerships in which families are respected as experts about their own children and recognized for their ability to support learning regardless of language or education levels.

Student Benefits

Students in particular reap many benefits when families are actively and consistently engaged across all levels of schooling (Weiss et al., 2018). Academic benefits from family–school collaboration include higher grades, higher standardized test scores, enrollment in more challenging courses, higher graduation rates, and greater enrollment in postsecondary education. Additional benefits of family partnerships include better attendance, improved behavior in school and at home, and lower rates of juvenile arrest. Students whose families are engaged also show more resilience and ability to persevere even in the face of obstacles.

Family Benefits

Families derive many benefits from partnerships with schools. School engagement allows families to connect with other families in the school community and build supportive relationships. This is especially important for immigrant families who may not be familiar with the US school system. Such relationships provide a means for families to make new friends and become better informed about the school system and how it operates. It also encourages families to learn about and access community resources. School engagement affords the opportunity for personal growth for family members. They may improve their skills through adult education, English classes, and library use. Such engagement has been found to increase families' self-confidence in their ability to interact with schools and support their child's school efforts (Wood & Bauman, 2017).

Teacher Benefits

Teachers often see the benefits of family engagement for the children or the families but don't realize that having families engaged can make their job easier, too. A hospitalized grandmother may result in a child being withdrawn or tired during school. Without good communication with the family, teachers may assume that the child simply doesn't want to listen or participate in school. When teachers are aware of family situations, they can make appropriate accommodations. Students need to know that families and teachers are on the same team rather than being pitted against each other.

Schoolwide Benefits

The school organization also derives many benefits from family engagement (Hanover Research, 2018). Schools that have high levels of family engagement benefit from the increased level of trust between the school and families. Such schools report that parents have more confidence in the school and rank teachers higher. Additionally, these schools report higher levels of morale among teachers, better parental understanding of the role of the teacher, and a high level of respect for parents as the child's first teacher. Schools with engaged families enjoy a better reputation in the community.

Schools benefit most when families are engaged in activities that support student achievement (Weiss et al., 2018). Research is clear that schools and families that work together see many benefits. Schools must reach out to linguistically and culturally diverse families in a variety of ways that allow families and the school to be valued partners in student success.

Challenges to Family Engagement

Almost all families, including immigrants, want the best education possible for their children but immigrant families face special challenges in engaging with schools. In a review of 40 studies, Antony-Newman (2019) found three major obstacles to immigrant family engagement: A mismatch between immigrant and teacher expectations for family engagement, language barriers, and a lack of teacher preparation.

Differing Expectations

Most immigrant families in the studies had expectations for family engagement arising from their experiences with schools in their native nations. This usually meant they saw their primary role as helping their children at home. For example, a study of Salvadoran immigrant parents found that the parents saw their role in their children's education as providing a good environment at home so their children could focus on their schooling and wouldn't have to worry about other things (Colón, 2017). This included providing food, housing, personal hygiene, and technology, and being a good role model. Many schools do not value this support at home. They expect families to participate in school activities, including meetings and fund-raising efforts. "Differences in expectations create mutual mis-communication which adversely affects children's learning" (Antony-Newman, 2019, p. 13).

Language Barriers

Language is another major barrier to immigrant family engagement. Studies have shown that parents who do not speak English fluently are viewed as less competent and less able to help their children academically despite their real capabilities (Antony-Newman, 2019). The U.S. Department of Justice and U.S. Department of Education (2015) issued a fact sheet explaining that schools must provide language assistance for families that request it even if the student is proficient in English. This is required for most school–family interactions, including registration, parent–teacher conferences, informational meetings, and much more. In addition, translation must be made by "appropriate and competent individuals" (p. 1), rather than students, siblings, or untrained school staff.

Lack of Educator Preparation

The third major challenge is a lack of educator preparation for family engagement. Research indicates that teachers and administrators do not receive sufficient preparation for partnering with families (Miller et al., 2013). They need professional development in engaging families, especially immigrant families. Educators, families, and community members all need to think in new ways to co-create environments for student success (Weiss et al., 2018). One way to increase involvement and awareness is to have immigrant families and community members provide in-service for teachers about what they do to support their students at home and how to make them feel more welcome at school (Gardner, 2019; see *Immigrant Family Panel* under activities).

Digital Divide

In addition to the three challenges to immigrant family engagement raised by Antony-Newman, the pandemic exposed technology challenges. Although statistics are not available for immigrant families specifically, 25 percent of US families with incomes under $30,000 lack computers (Auxier & Anderson, 2020). Some districts provided tablets or laptops for students, but they still lacked high-speed internet. A study by Microsoft in 2018 estimated that 163 million people in the United States lacked high-speed internet for video conferencing or streaming (Mansfield & Conlon, 2020). This has an impact on families' ability to access school information, communicate with educators, and assist their children with homework.

Educator Professional Development

Family engagement programs historically have focused on the school providing information to families and families volunteering at the school. The emphasis has now shifted to two-way communication, shared decision-making, and partnerships for student success. This book offers many activities that can be used for professional development and family engagement. Individuals, schools, and districts have different needs, but educators and administrators should consider these three broad topics.

- ◆ awareness
- ◆ communication
- ◆ respect

Self-Awareness

While 25 percent of students come from immigrant families, only 7 percent of K-12 teachers are immigrants (Furuya et al., 2019). This makes it all the more important for educators to become more attuned to their own beliefs as well as those of families. Yet, many times, it is difficult to pinpoint one's own beliefs or how they might differ from other people's until confronted with those differing expectations and beliefs. Many areas differ among cultures and may impact family engagement: the role of the teacher in education and behavior management, the role of the family in the child's education and behavior at school, the importance of individual achievement versus teamwork, the emphasis placed on teaching English or the home language at school, the belief in fate or hard work as the cause of success, and the way time is treated (Lynch & Hanson, 2004).

Awareness of Immigrant Families

In addition to being aware of one's own beliefs, it is important to understand some of the major cultural attitudes of the students' families. All families want the best for their children but what they consider to be the best and how to achieve it may differ from the views of the school. In her memoir, Hamid (2020) discusses how her Pakistani parents would not allow her to participate in coed school events, including field trips and swimming classes. They even were upset if a boy called on the phone about a group assignment. She says, "I know a lot of new immigrants have certain views about how the genders should interact with each other, especially families that are from conservative cultures" (personal communication, November 22, 2020). The students are then caught between home and school expectations.

The differences in expectations between families and schools may challenge effective family engagement. For example, many Mexicans have high regard for their teachers' knowledge and skills. They think it would seem rude or presumptuous to ask questions about what happens in school or to try to teach their children at home. But American teachers who are not accustomed to this belief and expect families to be more engaged in their children's education often see this respect as indifference.

Educators also need to be careful not to lump all immigrant families or even all families from one cultural group into one category. Immigrant families vary greatly just as other families vary. Some families are limited to one or two parents and a child, while others have support from extended families, including grandparents, aunts, and uncles. Some parents have been divorced or divorced and remarried. Children may live with relatives other than their parents. Some families have high levels of education, while others have had little opportunity to go to school. Some families may have disabilities that require special accommodations for communication. Beliefs about education and child rearing vary, also.

Additional differences are present among immigrants. The number of years the families have been in the United States and their acculturation differ. Some families have friends or other family members who understand the US education system, while others have to figure out the system on their own. Since most immigrant families have only been in the United States for a few years, their expectations of schools, teachers, and parenting are more likely to reflect their home culture than those of the families who have lived in the United States all their lives.

Although some immigrant families come to the United States for high-paying professional jobs, many are escaping poverty in their home countries and also face poverty here. Others had professional positions in their home countries but had to leave because of persecution, war, or other dangers. If they are not proficient in English or lack US certification in their fields, many immigrants have to accept manual labor jobs and work long hours to make ends meet. Salvadoran immigrants in the Washington D.C. area told Colón (2017) that educators don't understand everything they went through to get to the United States or how difficult it is to support their families and learn English at the same time. Some families barely have enough money for food and shelter. These families may not come to school because they cannot afford to lose wages, they lack reliable transportation, they need to use public transportation, or they need to pay for someone to take care of babies or toddlers. Families living in poverty also move more often in search of work and affordable housing, thus making it more difficult to develop ties with schools. Despite these limitations, most parents still care deeply about their children's education.

Care must be taken in assuming all families from similar ethnic backgrounds are the same. An example of cultural and linguistic differences among families who may appear to be similar can be found in the authors' own work with a family literacy program along the Texas–Mexico border (Sutterby et al., 2007). Although almost all the families engaged were Hispanic and lived in the same neighborhood, a close examination revealed many differences in family backgrounds within the program. Their situations included:

- ◆ recent immigrants from Mexico
- ◆ recent immigrants from Central America
- ◆ born and raised in the United States
- ◆ Spanish spoken at home
- ◆ English and Spanish spoken at home
- ◆ college-educated parents
- ◆ parents with little formal schooling
- ◆ varying levels of access to children's books

These differences might have been overlooked if the assumption was made that since the families were all Hispanic, they were alike.

Becoming aware of current attitudes about families, especially culturally and linguistically diverse families, is an important first step in understanding how to increase the engagement with immigrant families. The *Attitudes about Family Engagement Activity* at the end of the chapter can help raise awareness of everyone's views.

Communication

Families can offer valuable information to teachers about students' health, previous education, interests, and other issues that may impact their experience in school. If two-way communication exists, educators and administrators can also become more aware of the expectations, strengths, and needs of the families. When the family does not speak English, and the teacher does not speak the home language, two-way communication can be challenging, but federal law requires limited English proficiency families be given meaningful access to school information, services, and programs. For simple messages about upcoming events or class activities, the child can be used as an interpreter, but for more complex messages, someone outside the family is necessary.

Many families want to become more engaged in their children's education, but they simply don't know how. Some also believe that they cannot help because they do not speak English well. In these cases, the schools must make an extra effort to reach out to the families and communicate that their knowledge and efforts to support their children's education are valued.

Respect

Sometimes schools don't value everything families do to support students, especially activities at home. Gardner (2020) says there are two key principles in developing respect for immigrant families. Remember "parents have the capacity to help their children regardless of their background" and "parents are their child's first teacher and are experts on their children" (p. 1).

In a webinar on family engagement, Nesloney (2020) said that families, staff, and students will all become more engaged in building relationships when they feel "valued, empowered, and important." As a principal, he prioritized showing all families, students, and staff that they were truly welcome in the school community.

Families have skills and knowledge that they share with their children even if it is not what is generally considered *school learning*. For example, some families may not read books to their children, but they may tell stories, helping their children understand how stories are developed and increasing their children's vocabulary in their native language. Other families may teach their children skills, such as using herbs to treat illness, fixing cars, repairing plumbing, or writing in their home language. Teachers and schools can build upon the children's home knowledge and experiences to help the student succeed in school. By valuing home knowledge, teachers can help establish relationships with families that are built on respect.

> *When relationships with educators are characterized by mutual respect, trust, open communication, and inclusion in decision-making, families are more likely to feel confident about their roles as advocates and become more engaged in their children's learning. Positive relationships between educators and families even benefit children's health, social and emotional well-being, and cognitive skills.*
>
> (Weiss et al., 2018, p. 12)

Many of the activities and ideas in this book can be used with everyone from pre-service teachers to veteran administrators to build their capacity to successfully engage all families, including those who are culturally and linguistically diverse. The following activities can be used as part of faculty and staff meetings throughout the year.

Activity: Attitudes about Family Engagement

Purpose: This activity allows schools to investigate the attitudes of different stakeholders about family engagement and find out which types of family–school interactions each group values.

Participants: Families, teachers, administrators, school staff, community members, and middle school and high school students. Efforts should be made to collect information from as many people as possible, including secretaries, bus drivers, and custodians.

Preparation and resources: Decisions should be made about what questions will be asked, what forms of communication will be used, who will participate in the study, how the findings will be analyzed, and how the results will be reported and to whom.

Description of activity:

Questions. Schools can choose from the following questions or make up their own, but it is important that all stakeholders receive the same questions so that responses from different stakeholders can be compared.

◆ What should families do to support their children's education?
◆ What should teachers/schools do to communicate with families?
◆ What types of activities/meetings should teachers/schools have that engage families?
◆ What are the benefits of having families engaged in schools?
◆ What should the teachers and the school do when a child repeatedly misbehaves at school or receives poor grades?
◆ What should the family do when their child repeatedly misbehaves at school or receives poor grades?
◆ What do you think is the strongest part of children's education at this school?
◆ If you could improve one thing at this school, what would it be?

Methods of collecting information. Written and online surveys allow respondents to remain anonymous and are usually easier to analyze than personal interviews, but many families may be reluctant or unable (because of lack of technology) to answer online surveys. In order to make sure immigrant families are included in the responses, it may be necessary to meet with them in small groups and in their neighborhoods, such as at community centers or churches. Although this requires extra work, it may help educators receive responses from families who don't participate in traditional family events, such as open houses or parent teacher organizations.

Analysis and planning. If the effort is made to do an investigation, then the results should be analyzed and used for planning. How are school results similar or different from family or community responses? Results should also be compared to what is known about the benefits of different family engagement activities. For example, movie nights may develop a feeling of community and bring families to the school who would not otherwise be engaged. But movie nights are unlikely to directly impact student achievement or school–family communication. Therefore, efforts should be made to include a wide range of family engagement activities in any plan.

Options: Share the results with school organizations, such as Parent Teacher Association (PTA) and community organizations interested in increasing and diversifying family engagement.

Activity: Immigrant Family Panel

Purpose: This activity is designed to provide educators with more information about immigrant families that are part of their school community in order to improve family engagement. This is particularly important if there has been a shift in the demographics of the school in recent years.

Participants: Educators and a panel of three to five parents representing one immigrant group. An interpreter/translator.

Preparation and resources: Prepare a few questions and distribute them to the family representatives in advance in their home language.

Possible questions: How do you support your child's education at home? What were the schools in your home country like? What would you like us to know about your culture? How can the school better support your child's success? What could the school do better to communicate with families?

Description of activity: A facilitator should ask the panelists the prepared questions. Depending on time issues, you may want to tell participants in advance that everyone will not be asked to answer each question. Start with a different person for each question and then, if time allows, ask the other panelists if they have something to add. Limiting answers to a specific time limit might be considered rude in some cultures. Leave time at the end for educators to ask additional questions. If headsets are available, the interpreter can be just a few words behind the panelists or teachers asking questions. If they are not available, ask the interpreter to explain the main points of the panelists for the teachers and have a recorded transcript translated after the panel discussion.

Options: At a future meeting, educators can discuss the panel discussion and what it means for family engagement efforts, student education, curriculum, or behavior management. The first discussion may be with a new immigrant group or with the largest immigrant group attending the school. Future panel discussions can be with other immigrant groups. Panel discussions can be recorded with the participants' permission and shared with other families, school groups such as Parent Teacher Organization (PTO) and community organizations

Relevant Literature

Borderland Between Worlds: A Memoir, by Ayesha F. Hamid (2020), describes her immigrant experience growing up in the United States as a Pakistani child and woman. She was often caught between the culture of her family and the school, where she was bullied for being different. Despite her many challenges, Hamid believes immigrants offer hope to the world because they can provide bridges between cultures. *Chapter book.*

A Different Pond, by Bao Phi and illustrated by Thi Bui (2017), describes a fishing trip of a boy and his father who is an immigrant/refugee from Vietnam. The pond in the story mirrors a pond that the father fished in when he was young in Vietnam. The story discusses the hard work that this immigrant family has to do to survive in the United States, including fishing for food rather than for leisure. The child in the story learns to appreciate the culture of his family as he learns to adapt to the U.S. culture. *Picture book.*

Front Desk, by Kelly Yang (2018), describes the experiences of a young girl of Chinese immigrant parents who agree to take over the management of a hotel. The story focuses on the struggles many immigrants have when they are exploited by employers in the United States who take advantage of their immigrant status. The nexus of the story is the support groups that are formed to assist these immigrants overcome the obstacles of being an immigrant in the United States. The sequel, *Three Keys* (2020), continues the theme with the addition of a family from Mexico. *Chapter book.*

References

Antony-Newman, M. (2019). Parental involvement of immigrant parents: A meta-synthesis. *Educational Review*, 71(3), 362–381. https://doi.org/10.1080/00131911.2017.1423278

Auxier, B. & Anderson, M. (2020, March 16). *As schools close due to the coronavirus, some U.S. students face a digital 'homework gap'*. Pew Research Center. https://www.pewresearch.org/fact-tank/2020/03/16/as-schools-close-due-to-the-coronavirus-some-u-s-students-face-a-digital-homework-gap

Cohn, D. (2015, October 5). *Future immigration will change the face of America by 2065*. Pew Research Center. https://www.pewresearch.org/fact-tank/2015/10/05/future-immigration-will-change-the-face-of-america-by-2065/

Colón, I. T. (2017). *Los recién llegados: Construyendo collaborative relationships between recently arrived Salvadoran parents and educators in the nation's capital.*

Doctoral dissertation, Loyola University Chicago. https://ecommons. luc.edu/cgi/viewcontent.cgi?article=3789&context=luc_diss

Every Student Succeeds Act, 20 U.S.C. § 6301. (2015). https://www.congress. gov/114/plaws/publ95/PLAW-114publ95.pdf

Furuya, Y., Nooraddini, M. I., Wang, W., & Waslin, M. (2019, January). *A portrait of foreign-born teachers in the United States.* George Mason University Institute for Immigration Research. https://d101vc9winf8ln.cloudfront. net/documents/29869/original/Teacher_Paper_FINAL_WebVersion_ 012219.pdf?1548268969

Gardner, L. (2019, September 21). *10 possible alternatives to "international night".* Immigrant Connections. https://www.immigrantsrefugeesandschools. org/post/10-possible-alternatives-to-international-night

Gardner, L. (2020, March 26). *English learner family engagement during coronavirus.* Immigrant Connections. https://www.immigrantsrefugeesandschools. org/post/english-learner-family-engagement-during-coronavirus

Hamid, A. F. (2020). *The borderland between worlds: A memoir.* Auctus Publishers.

Hanover Research. (2018, November 8). *Top benefits of family and community engagement.* https://www.hanoverresearch.com/insights-blog/top- benefits-of-family-and-community-engagement/

Hornby, G. & Blackwell, I. (2018). Barriers to parental involvement in education: An update. *Educational Review*, 70(1), 109–119. https://doi.org/ 10.1080/00131911.2018.1388612

Lynch, E. W. & Hanson, M. J. (2004). *Developing cross-cultural competence: A guide for working with children and their families* (3rd ed.). Paul H. Brookes.

Mansfield, E. & Conlon, S. (2020, April 4). Coronavirus for kids without internet: Quarantine worksheets, learning in parking lots. *USA Today.* https://www.usatoday.com/story/news/education/2020/04/01/ coronavirus-internet-speed-broadband-online-learning-school-closures/ 5091051002/

Miller, G. E., Lines, C., Sullivan, E., & Hermanutz, K. (2013). Preparing educators to partner with families. *Teaching Education*, 24(2), 150–163. https:// doi.org/10.1080/10476210.2013.786889

National Center for Education Statistics. (2020). *English language learners in public schools. The condition of public education 2020.* https://nces.ed.gov/ programs/coe/pdf/coe_cgf.pdf

Nesloney, T. (2020). *Family engagement: How to build relationships by tearing down walls.* [Webinar] Livingtree. Retrieved January 3, 2021 from https:// try.livingtree.com/webinar-recording/how-to-build-relationships-by- tearing-down-walls/

Office of English Language Acquisition. (2020, February). *English learners: Demographic trends.* National Clearinghouse for English Language

Acquisition. https://ncela.ed.gov/files/fast_facts/19-0193_Del4.4_ELDemographicTrends_021220_508.pdf

Sutterby, J. A., Rubin, R., & Abrego, M. (2007). Amistades: The development of relationships between preservice teachers and Latino families. *School Community Journal*, 17(1), 77–94. http://www.adi.org/journal/ss07/SutterbyRubinAbregoSpring2007

Urban Institute. (2019, March 14). *Part of us: A data driven look at children of immigrants*. https://www.urban.org/features/part-us-data-

U.S. Department of Justice & U.S. Department of Education. (2015). *Information for limited English proficient (LEP) parents and guardians and for schools and school districts that communicate with them*. https://www2.ed.gov/about/offices/list/ocr/docs/dcl-factsheet-lep-parents-201501.pdf

Weiss, H. B., Lopez, M. E, & Caspe, M. (2018, October 23). *Carnegie challenge paper: Joining together to create a bold vision for next generation family engagement*. Global Family Research Project. https://globalfrp.org/content/download/419/3823/file/GFRP_Family%20Engagement%20Carnegie%20Report.pdf

Wood, L. & Bauman, E. (2017, February). *How family, school, and community engagement can improve student achievement and influence school reform: Literature review*. American Institutes for Research and Nellie Mae Education Foundation. https://cursoslared.com/recursoslibre/Final-Report-Family-Engagement-AIR.pdf

2

Finding Out What Families Want

Scenario: Investigating What Families Want

Hudde was president of the PTA (Parent Teacher Association) at Roosevelt Middle School in Austin, Texas. She was well-known for her boundless energy for participating at school. She visited the school nearly every day. She and her husband have lived in the same house two blocks from the school for nearly 20 years. The youngest of her six children was in middle school.

Hudde's work as president of the PTA made her indispensable to the school. The principal relied on PTA for sponsoring teacher celebrations such as Welcome Back to School and Teacher Appreciation Week. The PTA also raised funds for beautification projects around the school and provided refreshments for the *Preparing for High School Night* sponsored by the counseling department.

Fundraising was Hudde's strong suit. She had endless energy to ask for donations from local businesses. These were used as door prizes at the annual bingo night, which brought in the majority of funds for the PTA. The bingo night fundraiser brought out nearly 1,500 participants to the school. Families from across the school took part. Groups of family and community members could be heard speaking Spanish, Vietnamese, and English while playing bingo.

The enthusiasm of the bingo night didn't transfer to other school activities planned for parents. Back to School Night and PTA general membership meetings were sparsely attended. And even when PTA had sponsored a new event, *morning coffee with the principal*, only seven parents attended. Three of the seven attendees were officers on the PTA board and English was the only language spoken at the coffee.

When Hudde first moved to the neighborhood, it was almost all single-family homes of professionals and workers in the local technology industry. Now, these families had moved away or had seen their children grow up and leave home. Numerous homeowners had been replaced with renters from all corners of the world; many from Mexico, but also from El Salvador, Honduras, and Vietnam. Street signs were printed in both Vietnamese and English.

Ms. McGruder, the school principal, had been at the school for eight years and had witnessed the school's demographic shift from a majority white to a majority minority population. She hired as many bilingual teachers as she could get and employed two Vietnamese aides and a Vietnamese-speaking secretary. Still, she worried about communication and lack of parent participation in the school. She had noticed that nearly all PTA members at the school were white women, parent school meetings were held in English, and school events were poorly attended with the exception of the annual bingo night. The school spirit and sports programs along with the theater program had few of the newer immigrants as participants.

Ms. Mc Gruder wondered how she could translate the enthusiasm of the bingo night to other activities at school. Was limited parent participation typical of middle school or was there something else that could be done? She scheduled a conversation with Hudde about what they might do to increase family participation at Roosevelt's events. Hudde decided the best way to find out what the parents wanted from the school was to investigate. With that, Hudde, with her famed energy for taking on difficult projects, was off to find out the best way to gather information about what families wanted.

Family Needs Assessments

Most schools think they do a good job reaching out to families. If asked how well they work with parents, schools will usually respond that they communicate fairly well and even offer several ways for parents to be involved in school life. Open houses, parent teacher conferences, reading and math strategy nights, homework help night, volunteer opportunities, and invitations to join parent teacher organizations are often identified.

These outreach activities may have little use for some families, especially those who are immigrants and culturally and linguistically diverse. Does your school know what parents think about your school outreach efforts? How does your school find out what families want and need from the school?

Scenario: Differing Expectations

The following is an actual conversation with a mother who had recently immigrated to the United States from Mexico with her four children. The parent was the mother of a child in the first-grade classroom of one of the author's graduate students. The mother was asked, "How have you been involved with the school as a whole, the principal, and the teacher?" The mother responded in Spanish with a description of her one and only attempt to attend a school parent teacher organization meeting:

> We went one time to a meeting where there were several parents present, but we got up and left. The meeting was in English, and there was an argument. I think that they were attacking one another, and it just did not sound good. We do not like arguments. We had all the kids with us, and people (teachers and parents) were staring at us, so we left. We do not want to go to something like that again. [Translated from Spanish into English]

The same mother went on to describe another attempt at being involved with the school by going to a parent teacher conference:

> We were invited one time to a parent conference to tell us that my son was not following the rules. We talked to my son, but we were still working on it. He had all S's on his report card, except for discipline. He is still having a hard time learning to follow the rules. We were never invited back because we [the family] all went, and my kids were upsetting the teacher. [Translated from Spanish into English]

Traditional school events such as a PTO (Parent Teacher Organization) meeting and a parent teacher conference proved to be unfamiliar and negative experiences for this mother. Chances are this parent will never attend another PTO meeting or come back for a parent teacher conference. How will the school ever know why she did not return or how she feels?

It is important that schools find a way to obtain input and feedback from all families, including those who may be unintentionally excluded by *traditional* outreach activities. A critical part of family outreach is finding out what *all* parents want and providing parents with opportunities to let the school know what they can do better. This can be especially challenging when working with immigrant families who may be unfamiliar with American schooling and face language barriers.

Surveys

Many different types of surveys are administered to families. Some are administered by most schools every year, such as surveys to identify families' preferred language of communication and mode of communication such as text, email, and phone app. Surveys also can be used to determine devices and connectivity in the home for communication and home learning.

For example, during the 2020 COVID 19 Pandemic, family surveys helped some schools identify the technology support needed when face-to-face instruction quickly transitioned to 100% online in the home. Schools making use of surveys were able to determine if families needed access to computing hardware and or internet connectivity. Results from the survey allowed school districts to distribute computers, tablets, mobile hotspots, etc. Additionally, surveys were utilized to help school districts plan reopening efforts. Schools during the pandemic needed to find out if families needed children at school so they could return to work or if they preferred to keep children at home to protect the family from a potential infection. Schools that were not able to utilize surveys were left to guess what families wanted or needed and, as a result, student learning suffered.

Satisfaction Surveys

Other types of surveys aim at finding levels of satisfaction with current practices. For example, surveys often ask families to rank how well the school keeps all families informed about important issues and events or how well a child's teacher keeps parents informed about how the child is doing in school. These surveys often list current practices such as parent teacher conferences and ask parents to rate their feelings about this practice as very dissatisfied to very satisfied. This type of survey does not help identify the specific practices that create satisfaction or dissatisfaction with the school. For example, a parent might say they are satisfied with parent teacher conferences, but it could be for many reasons, including length of the conference, scheduling options, the teacher's attitude, or a glowing report on their child. Surveys about current practices also fail to gain input about needs that are not currently being met.

Open-Ended Questions

In order to get more detailed input from families, it is important that surveys are in the family's home language and that at least some of the questions are open-ended to allow families to provide more detailed answers than "very satisfied." Families may be asked, "What would you like to learn more about related to your child's education?" For example, Washoe County Schools in Nevada stresses listening to the needs of the family and finding out how schools can best support learning in the home (personal communication, October 29, 2020). Portland Empowered, a family leadership initiative, allows families to select topics and lead dialogue with school officials as opposed to schools selecting the topics to be discussed (personal communication, October 13, 2020). It is too easy for schools to plan out family engagement activities for the year based on what they think parents need. Far too often assumptions are made about the needs of diverse families that may not at all be what families want. There is a difference between soliciting input on how well a school shares information it has decided parents should know and gathering information from all families about what they would like to learn about the school or how the school could support their parenting efforts.

Providing Background Information

Parenting materials frequently suggest the need to gather parental input on specific school policies or curriculum revisions, such as school uniforms or year-round schooling. Although family input is important on these issues, it is vital to make sure that families are well informed on the various advantages and disadvantages before soliciting family input. This might be done through forums held in community centers, churches, or other gathering points as well as in the school. For example, some school districts began year-round schools with the backing of the parents only to find them opposing the innovation a few years later (Chen, 2020). Before the year-round schools began, the families did not understand that year-round schools usually have weeks off in fall or spring when other schools are in session. This makes finding childcare for young school-aged children difficult.

Appropriate Survey Topics

There also may be some topics that are not appropriate for family surveys or are appropriate for only some families. For example, most parents do not have the experience or knowledge to compare one reading or math program with another. One school survey asked all parents about the exit exam given to high school seniors. If families did not have a child who had already taken the exit exam, their opinions were unlikely to be well-informed. Specific surveys can be created for different families. For example, the families of seniors could receive a survey about how well prepared their child was for the exit exam, graduation, and the future. This survey could also solicit ideas for ways of better preparing future students. Families who just registered a child in the school district could receive surveys about the registration process.

Well-intentioned surveys to gather parent feedback may actually serve to marginalize culturally and linguistically diverse families. A PTA at an elementary school gave an online survey to its parents related to PTA efforts to support the school. Each item on the survey was to be ranked as a priority, acceptable, or not a concern. Areas surveyed included school bookfairs, classroom volunteers, Dr. Seuss's birthday celebration, field day, teachers' Christmas wish lists, and e-mail as a means of communicating with the PTA. The survey was well intentioned but would be meaningless for families unfamiliar with American schooling and culture and those who did not speak English.

Culturally and linguistically diverse families could possibly be labeled as unsupportive of efforts to improve the school if they did not participate in the survey. The reality is that these parents want their children to succeed in school but may not know how to participate in the manner the school wants or expects.

Digital Survey Tools

Digital tools exist to help schools to administer family surveys. The website Capterra offers a comparison of product features for various online software (see references). Schools using the site can identify survey software that fits their needs. Survey Monkey offers a K-12 parent template that schools may find helpful (see references). The advantage of digital tools is the ease in data collection and organization.

Panorama Education helps schools and districts collect valid and reliable feedback from families. A free tool on its site is the *Family School Relationships Survey* (Panorama Education, n.d.). The survey is designed to provide schools with a clear picture of family attitudes about various key topics. For example, the barriers to engagement section examines factors that create challenges for families to interact or become involved with their child's school. A campus or district may use this information to improve its family engagement efforts. The survey is available in ten different languages that may be downloaded directly from their site.

Although using digital tools may be convenient for schools, schools need to be aware that the survey data may predominantly reflect the views of those families who feel very comfortable with the school. Families who are less comfortable or familiar with the school or with technology, such as immigrant families, are probably not equally represented in the data.

Equitable Data Collection

The Equitable Parent School Research Project (EPSRP) at the University of Washington offers lessons learned about the process of developing and administering family surveys to ensure equitable representation of all families in the school community. Such guidance is especially useful for schools with immigrant families who might otherwise be left out by traditional survey approaches.

Schools should begin by putting together a culturally inclusive leadership team, representative of all families, that will work through the entire survey process from beginning to end. Schools should invite community partners and parent leaders from underserved communities to serve on the team. This allows the leadership team to learn about all the families they serve as they plan the survey. Community leaders have a wealth of knowledge to help schools better understand unique issues and needs facing the families they represent (Eller & Eller, 2018). This results in meaningful issues being added to the survey that might otherwise have been overlooked.

The EPSRP also shares specific lessons learned related to the logistics of survey administration. Schools should consider incorporating these suggestions to ensure survey data is representative of all families, particularly immigrant families. Highlights of general lessons learned from the EPSRP include the following items.

◆ Administer family surveys in late fall or early winter within a three-to-six-week window that doesn't conflict with other activities. This allows the school year to start and families to have interacted with teachers.

◆ Make the survey available both online and in a paper format. Paper surveys can be handed directly to families and allow for completion in more than one sitting. Many families prefer paper surveys.

◆ Work with teachers, aides, and parent leaders to identify the languages needed for the survey and the appropriate literacy level.

◆ Stress to families that the survey is not a test and the results are confidential and anonymous.

◆ Utilize culturally relevant data collection strategies such as having parent leaders organize small gatherings with families in their neighborhood or apartment buildings to fill out surveys; organizing events in school with bilingual–bicultural facilitators to complete surveys in groups; and reach out to families at drop-off and pick-up times at school and in community after-school programs to encourage survey completion and to collect surveys.

The project also stressed the importance of community and parent leaders representative of underserved communities or cultural brokers' availability during the survey administration period. Cultural brokers and community leaders can use their networks to encourage participation in the survey and to answer questions from families about how to fill out the survey. They can assist in collecting paper surveys and ensure they remain anonymous.

As mentioned earlier, the EPSRP encourages the stakeholders (community leaders, parent leaders, and cultural brokers) to be part of the survey administration process from beginning to end. Therefore, once data is gathered, the leadership team should gather together to examine the data and make sense of it. The project suggests the following questions be asked of the team about the data: "Were we surprised by the data? What does the data tell us? What does the data not tell us? What other questions do we have? What else do we need to know?" (The Equitable Parent School Collaboration Research Project, 2015, p. 13). The questions allow the school to explore the survey data from multiple perspectives. For example, parent leaders may focus on different aspects of the data than school officials. If the school had interpreted the data alone with no stakeholder input, these points of view may have gone unnoticed or unheard. Schools should take action on the data by working with stakeholders to collectively prioritize what is most important from the data. These priorities can then be turned into action steps for the school.

Schools must make it a priority to learn from all families. The perspectives of *hard-to-reach families* on family engagement efforts will yield valuable information on how to improve such efforts and build meaningful partnerships. The time and effort invested by the school to hear from all families is worth it as it yields data that truly represents what all families want from the school. Administering surveys is not merely something a school does to comply with a checklist of family engagement activities, it is about engaging families in continuous improvement. Families that see the school values their input and follows up on concerns are more likely to continue and even increase their engagement with the school.

Beyond Surveys

Methods other than traditional surveys about existing school practices should be used by schools so that input is collected from all families. Teachers may ask parents in person what topics they would like to learn about. This information can be asked of parents when students are dropped off in the morning, picked up from school, or at any time the opportunity presents itself. People are often more honest when they are not putting things down in writing. Such feedback allows the school to identify the information and services that all families want and need.

For example, one time we (the authors) were working with a local elementary school on an afterschool reading program. Various literacy topics were considered for families. It would be easy to assume that since the families did not speak English, were recent immigrants, and came from high-poverty households that literacy practices did not take place in the home and perhaps parents themselves needed to learn to read and write or be shown how to read to their children and make books available for them. However, in talking with the parents over several weeks, parents expressed a strong interest in the states' early literacy assessment being used in the school and wanted to learn about what it was and how it would be used to monitor their children's progress. It is unlikely that this information would have been gathered from a written or online survey sent out to families.

School office staff can be trained to solicit information from families about their needs when students are registered for school, picked up for doctor's appointments, and so on. Parent liaisons can also serve as valuable resources in helping obtain information from parents, including suggestions for how the school can better meet their needs. Such conversations with school staff send the message that the school is open and receptive to parental input from all families.

Parents themselves can help obtain information from other families. Find families who are willing to contact other families with children in the same school and collect information from them. In this way, information may be obtained from families who do not come to the school or complete written surveys. Some schools use parent volunteers who are willing to give out their phone number so that families may call them with questions about school. Parent volunteers can keep track of questions and concerns and share them with the school.

Administrators can solicit information from families when various types of meetings are held such as PTA meetings, parent coffees, and home visits. Principals may even consider hosting an activity such as lunch with the principal with the specific purpose of hearing from families about the topics they are interested in learning.

Some schools also solicit information from middle school and high school students. In this way, the school can find out about what the students may be telling their families about teaching, discipline, homework, and student relations.

Focus Groups

Focus groups are another way of soliciting information from families. This is a method of gathering information used by private marketing firms that can also be applied in schools. An informal group of 6 to 12 family members may be chosen for their specific knowledge or background. For example, a focus group could be formed with families of emergent bilinguals of Somali background and an interpreter could be present to moderate the discussion. General questions could be asked about what successes their children were having and what they thought might be improved. Participants respond not only to the moderator but also to each other. These informal discussions often elicit information that might not come to light on surveys or in one-on-one interviews. Of course, these focus groups only represent the opinions or beliefs of a small group of people, and some people may be afraid to discuss their true feelings because the discussions are being recorded or because of other members of the focus group.

Topics of Interest

It is important to ask general questions to find out about the needs and wishes of families and children without limiting them to issues that the school considers important. For example, families may be asked what the school could do better. The answers to this general question may include ideas that had not been previously considered by the school. For example, some families may want the school to be open 30 minutes earlier so they can bring their child to school before leaving for work, others may want a health clinic to be associated with the school, and still others may want their children to have music time and would be willing to volunteer their services to teach songs. Parents may want to know more about online teaching activities or the school online teaching portal such as Seesaw or Class Dojo. Each of these suggestions provides both challenges and opportunities that may not have previously been considered by the school.

In addition, the school may want to ask questions about specific topics of interest. These will vary from school to school, but some suggestions include homework, discipline, bullying, grading, extracurricular activities, transportation, safety, and communication.

Comprehensive Planning

Schools should develop a comprehensive plan or approach for conducting the family needs assessment in their school community. The initial step involves determining how well the school currently conducts needs assessments of families.

The activities at the end of the chapter will be helpful in making this determination. Additionally, the activities will help schools modify existing surveys and select appropriate formats for soliciting input from all families.

When possible, seek the assistance of community agencies, civic groups, and faith-based organizations in the school attendance area to plan, advertise, and implement the school's comprehensive needs assessment. These organizations may be able to conduct family focus groups for the school. They may also encourage and increase family participation in written surveys. Volunteers may offer to administer the surveys orally and record the results for families uncomfortable with writing. Diverse families may also feel more comfortable participating in the needs assessment outside the school setting in locations such as community centers, churches, temples, or mosques.

A timeframe for the needs assessment should be established and plans developed for how the data will be compiled and analyzed. Decide in advance if the district is able to provide support to the school on this step or if the services of an outside organization will be needed. The results of the needs assessment should be shared with the community in the appropriate languages and utilized to develop a plan of action to build a stronger relationship with all families, especially those that are from different cultural backgrounds.

Activity: Analyze School Needs Assessment Practices

Purpose: The purpose of this activity is to determine how well the school gathers and solicits information from all families in the school community, including those who are culturally and linguistically diverse.

Participants: School faculty and staff

Preparation and resources: Run off the list of questions below. Have copies of any current needs assessment the school uses available as a reference.

Description of activity: Assemble school staff and ask them the questions below in an effort to determine the current status of the campus in assessing the needs of all families. Divide the faculty and staff into small groups to review the questions. Each group should have a member assigned to record the responses. After each group has answered the questions, the responses should be shared with the entire group. At the closing of the discussion, arrangements should be made to analyze the responses, discuss them with staff members, and write a plan based on the information.

Does your campus conduct a needs assessment of families?

- If so, how is it done?
- Why is the needs assessment conducted? How are you reaching families who are not online?
- How and with whom are the results shared?
- What changes have occurred at your school as a result of the needs assessment?
- If the school conducts needs assessments, do families just comment on current practices or is there an opportunity to suggest new ideas or express concerns on different topics?
- What overall percentage of school families provide input regarding their wants and needs?
- To what extent are families of English language learners and immigrants a part of the overall percentage of family input?
- Describe the typical family in your school? Does one exist?
- Does your school hold expectations for family engagement that center around traditional mainstream families? Explain your response. (Recall that this question was posed in Chapter 1 when examining how each group of stakeholders may hold differing views regarding which benefits of family involvement are the most valued.)
- What changes need to be made to ensure that the needs and wants of all school families are integrated into the school and surrounding community?
- Whose responsibility is it to make changes that increase the involvement of all families, including those from different cultural backgrounds?

Options: Conduct the same activity with a cross section of stakeholders, including family members, community members, and staff. Compare the results of each group's discussion and use the results to help develop a comprehensive needs assessment for the campus.

Activity: Focus Groups

Purpose: Focus group interviews allow schools to obtain more in-depth information from selected families. Although more information is revealed in these group interviews than in most written surveys, as a practical matter fewer families can be contacted.

Participants: Family members from a particular cultural and linguistic group should be selected.

Preparation and resources: Prepare focus group questions in advance; identify school faculty or community members to conduct the interview and to record family responses. (A university may be helpful in providing someone who can interpret in the native language of the families being interviewed.)

Description of activity: A variety of questions may be asked of parents during the interviews. Here are some possibilities:

◆ In what family engagement opportunities/activities have you participated at your child's school? Describe your experience.
◆ What barriers exist that hold you back from participating more in your child's school?
◆ What suggestions do you have for how the school could increase family engagement?
◆ Is there anything else that you would like to tell us?

After the interviews are conducted, summarize the responses and share them with school faculty and staff. Use the information to determine what changes are needed in parental engagement efforts to reach out to all families. Repeat the focus group as needed to accommodate as many cultural and linguistic groups as are part of the school community.

Note of caution: Questions for the focus groups should be modified as needed to ensure they are culturally sensitive. Feedback should be solicited from a family or community member who represents the cultural and linguistic group being interviewed to assure questions are culturally sensitive.

Relevant Literature

Josias, Hold the Book, by Jennifer Riesmeyer Elvgren (2006), describes a boy growing up on a farm in Haiti. He has to work on the farm to help support his family, so he cannot go to school. Josias is responsible for growing beans in the garden but has difficulty doing it. In the end, he asks how school might help him learn to farm better. His family agrees to let him study in school so he can come back and help the family with the farm. *Picture book.*

We Came to America, by Faith Ringold (2016), looks at America's rich and difficult history of voluntary and involuntary immigration and diversity. A recurring refrain in the book is, "Every color, every race, and religion, from every country in the world. In spite of where we came from or how or why we came, We are all Americans just the same." The book highlights the unique gifts all immigrant cultures have brought to share with America and even though we or our ancestors have come from different places or were here to begin with, all of us are Americans. *Picture book.*

References

Capterra. (n.d.). *Survey Software.* https://www.capterra.com/p/72393/Survey-Methods/#comparisons

Chen, G. (2020, October 5). Year round or traditional schedule. *Public School Review.* https://www.publicschoolreview.com/blog/year-round-or-traditional-schedule

Eller, J. F. & Eller, S. A. (2018, March/April). Cultural competence for new principals. *Principal*, 97(4), 42–43.

The Equitable Parent School Collaboration Research Project. (2015). *User's guide for road map family engagement survey: Data inquiry for equitable collaboration.* University of Washington. https://education.uw.edu/sites/default/files/programs/epsc/Users%20Guide%20Road%20Map%20Survey.pdf

Panorama Education. (n.d.). *Family school relationships survey.* https://www.panoramaed.com/

Survey Monkey. (n.d.). *K-12 parent survey template.* https://www.surveymonkey.com/mp/k-12-parent-survey-template/

3

Creating a Welcoming School Environment

Scenario: All Families Welcome!

Irma Rosales was very excited about the upcoming school year. Just yester-day, two faculty members from the neighborhood school, Bluebonnet Elemen-tary, stopped by to greet the family and extend their wishes for a wonderful school year. Her local parish priest had announced at the church that staff from Bluebonnet Elementary School would be doing a neighborhood walk to meet families and share school information.

The teachers hadn't stayed long—only about ten minutes. They brought a *welcome gift* for the family—a folder embossed with the name of the school and important contact information, including phone numbers and e-mail addresses. They introduced Ms. Rosales to the school app that would allow them to communicate using their phones. In addition to the folder, the family received Bluebonnet's calendar for the year and a refrigerator magnet shaped like a school with important school phone numbers for easy access. All the information was published in both Spanish and English.

At the visit, the teachers explained in Spanish that they were doing a neighborhood walk and wanted to make sure that everyone knew when the first day of school was, how to register for school, and how to get in touch with the school if they had any questions. The teachers seemed genuinely interested in meeting her twins, Mary and Juan, who would be attending school for the first time. Mrs. Rosales was relieved to be able to ask some questions about the prekindergarten program. The teachers explained that Bluebonnet Elementary was able to help families make connections to community agencies and services. The teachers also took the time to ask what needs the school could assist her with and ask what topics she'd be interested in learning about related to the school.

Mrs. Rosales later thought about the information she had learned during the visit: how to register her children for school and the date Bluebonnet would host a *Meet the Teacher Saturday* prior to the school year starting. She was relieved that she would have the opportunity to see her children's classroom and meet her children's teachers before the school year started. Perhaps most of all, she was excited that the school had a school-based mobile health unit available to provide physicals and immunizations. The clinic would allow her to get the twins' immunizations up to date before the start of school. Her neighbors were right. The local elementary school loved and cared about its students. She could rest easier knowing that she could trust the school with her twins and was glad people at the school spoke Spanish.

Importance of School Climate

Mrs. Rosales's first encounter with Bluebonnet Elementary was very positive and productive. The school was able to furnish Mrs. Rosales with critical school information on ways to communicate, starting dates, events, and health services. Teachers asked questions and demonstrated a genuine interest in her children. It was clear that the school wanted families engaged as they came to her home and visited with the parish priest.

Bluebonnet Elementary sent out a clear message to Mrs. Rosales that families were important and valued by the school. Now, even before families came to the school building for the first time, they could be confident the school would be happy to see them and welcome them. Its outreach was deliberately and intentionally planned to engage families who did not speak English and or lacked familiarity with American schooling. Scheduling a Saturday back to school event versus a weekday or weeknight event was aimed at meeting the needs of working families. Bluebonnet Elementary School was ready and willing to build a relationship with its school community, including diverse families.

Making schools a welcoming place is critical to families who are culturally and linguistically diverse. Schools can be viewed as intimidating places at odds with families' native culture, language, and values or they can be viewed as welcoming places that help families and acknowledge diversity. Some immigrant families' native cultures, i.e., Hmong and Timm, may view teachers as educational experts and don't expect to be involved in their children's education. Some parents may have had little experience with formal schooling themselves and believe they are unable to guide their child's schooling. Still others fear being misunderstood or that their children will lose their home culture and language at school. Some Somali families, for example, fear that sending children to school will result in loss of the child's native language when they learn English (Ikhar, 2018).

Principals and teachers should consider writing a personal note to their students prior to the school year starting or holding an event such as Meet the Teacher Night. Many students may have never received a handwritten letter and are very excited to be personally welcomed to the school year. One campus increased their attendance at Meet the Teacher Night from 37 to 98% through letters (Nesloney, 2020). Handwritten letters serve as a friendly and personal invitation for families to come to the school. Letters are especially meaningful to immigrant families who might otherwise not attend a school event.

Welcoming schools do not ignore differences in language and culture. Instead, they acknowledge, learn about, honor, and value these differences. Schools wishing to engage families of immigrants must send a clear and sincere message that they are interested in partnering with them in a meaningful way to make schooling a successful experience. Schools convey such a message by providing a welcoming climate filled with positive interactions between the school and the family.

What Makes a Welcoming School?

Looking at your school through the eyes of an immigrant family who may be enrolling in American schools for the first time (or new to your district or campus) will help you create a more welcoming environment. It is important to remember that families have contact with a variety of school staff, not just family liaisons, teachers, and principals. Any efforts that are made to learn more about a school's climate should include secretaries, receptionists, guidance counselors, cafeteria workers, security guards, school nurses, librarians, custodians, crossing guards, bus drivers, and so on.

Take a minute to think about how an outsider might approach your school. What sort of knowledge would you need in order to access your school? What sort of information can you get from signs around campus, especially if you do not speak English? How are staff trained to greet visitors to the school? What sorts of routines like registration or vaccinations would families need to know? As insiders, we often assume the answers to these questions are simple, but often to outsiders, the answers are not so obvious.

Campuses can create a welcoming environment for families with something as simple as displaying photos showing the various student activities that take place at school. Visitors to the campus will get a glimpse into school life and students will enjoy seeing themselves too. Photos can be easily and inexpensively printed on canvas and hung in hallways around the school (Nesloney, 2020). Canvas prints can be saved and moved to different locations around the school each year. Schools should take care to ensure that its photos are representative of all cultures within their school and span all grade levels.

Immigrant Families and Orientation

Campuses wishing to be more sensitive and supportive to immigrant families should enhance their registration or *joining the school* process by offering a special orientation session designed to help immigrant families learn how U.S. schools work. Table 3.1 provides a listing of possible orientation topics aimed to make families more knowledgeable and comfortable with the culture of American schools. Well-planned and intentional orientation sessions help new immigrant families join school and feel welcome. A positive first experience lays a strong foundation for all future family engagement.

Orientations are commonly delivered at the start of the school year. However, schools will continue to register new families throughout the school year. Immigrant Connections suggests three possible delivery options that can be used all year long: (a) In person; (b) Handbook; and (c) Multilingual Video (English Learner Portal, 2019). Schools may find some combination of the three options the most useful in making new families feel welcomed by the school or district.

Delivering an in-person orientation session provides an opportunity to build relationships with families and to answer specific questions. Schools must determine what languages need interpretation and if childcare or transportation will be made available for families. This type of session may be difficult to offer multiple times during the year. Some districts like Portland, Maine, have a special welcoming and intake center for immigrant families and an orientation session may be offered there (Portland Public Schools, n.d.).

Schools may wish to create a handbook specifically designed for immigrant families that can be handed out when new families register throughout the year. Crawford Elementary in Aurora, Colorado, has created welcome books available in English, Spanish, Somali, Burmese, French, and Nepali

Table 3.1 Possible Orientation Topics

- Accessing school/district information online—websites, passwords for platforms, translation
- After-school activities—tutoring, clubs, and sports
- Attendance policy—mandatory phone call and note when child is sick
- Back to School Night information
- Cafeteria options—bring food or purchase meals/free and reduced lunch applications
- Class procedures—raising hand to speak, lining up to leave the classroom
- Coed classes
- Communicating and engaging with the school
- Course schedules—child will have more than one teacher and more than one classroom
- Discipline in the school context
- Dress code—wearing or not wearing a uniform, gym clothes
- Emergency drills
- Field trips
- Grading
- How students and teachers relate to and address one another
- Levels of school—elementary, middle, and high school—primarily based on age
- Lockers
- Parent–teacher conference dates and purpose
- Physical layout of the school
- Physical exams and immunizations
- Report cards
- Role of school personnel and who to go to with specific concerns
- School calendar—school begins in August or September and not January
- School safety and sign-in procedures
- Sitting still for long periods of time
- Special education services
- Summer school availability
- Transportation—school buses are yellow and for students only; how to ride on the bus

(Bridging Refugee Youth and Children's Services, n.d.-b; English Learner Portal 2019, n.d.; Short & Boyson, 2012; U.S. Department of Education, 2017;)

(Crawford Elementary, n.d.). The welcome book includes pictures of the school, main office, and school personnel such as the school secretary, librarian, and gym and art teachers. School procedures are explained with simple sentences and photos illustrating the school day. Students are given the books to keep and refer to as needed.

A third delivery option to offer families is a multilingual orientation video. Classroom teachers may also wish to make short videos filming classroom routines specific to their class to share with parents (Warsi, 2017). A parent group may be able to enlist community members to help with narrating the video into the languages needed. A major advantage of making an orientation video is that it can be placed on a school's website to be accessed by families throughout the year. It may also be helpful for immigrant families who may not read and write in their native language.

It is important that schools and districts keep in mind that federal law requires schools to provide information in a language families can understand. Details are described in an Office of Civil Rights (OCR) document titled, *Information for Limited English Proficient (LEP) Parents and Guardians and for Schools and School Districts that Communicate with them* (The U.S. Department of Justice & U.S. Department of Education's Office for Civil Rights, 2015). More information about communicating with families in their home language can be found in Chapter 4.

Evaluating the School Environment

Schools may wish to use a *Mystery Shopper* to evaluate the school's interactions with families (see activity at the end of chapter). This means a visitor comes to the school to see how he or she is treated and determine to what extent the school climate is welcoming. Using a Mystery Shopper helps schools examine how visitors who do not speak English or are unfamiliar with American schooling are treated.

Fairfax County schools use a variation of the Mystery Shopper called the Welcoming Schools Process. Small teams of four to five people are assigned to a specific school to rate its friendliness. Team members conducting the evaluation should be culturally diverse and lack familiarity with the school. Each team member is given an area to assess such as school staff, physical environment, written materials, and practices and policies. The complete *How to Evaluate Your School* is available online (Underhill, 2014). The Houston Independent School District and the Kentucky Department of Education offer additional welcoming checklists for use (see references).

Results from the evaluation of the school's welcoming environment need to be shared with the school and may be used to build an action plan to make the school more welcoming to all families including those who bring different language needs and cultural experiences and are culturally and linguistically diverse.

Welcoming Atmosphere and Language

The ideal situation for any school is to have bilingual office staff who make emergent bilinguals feel welcome at their new school. However, the reality is that schools may need to be able to communicate in multiple languages. One of the authors recalls a weekday in which two students arrived at her school on a day with no classes. The office staff spoke English and Spanish, but not Haitian Creole.

Schools should be prepared to handle situations in which the office staff do not speak the language of the family. It may be best to have some standard phrases in several different languages with pronunciation guides, so the office staff can determine the language of the person speaking. New York Public Schools' Translation and Interpretation Unit offers 'I Speak' cards in which parents may point to the language which needs translation (Urdu, Haitian Creole, French, Korean, Spanish, Bengali, Russian, and Arabic) (New York City Department of Education, n.d.).

Once the needed language is determined, the appropriate interpretation service may be provided. The options include trained interpreters in person and by phone, bilingual colleagues, and translation apps (see Chapter 4). The bottom line is to make sure every staff member knows how to access appropriate language services to communicate with emergent bilingual families.

The standard phrases in different languages are also useful when answering the school phone as it is important to determine if the person calling has an emergency, and if not, take a number so someone who speaks the family's native language can call back later. Another alternative is to have a prerecorded message in several languages that asks the families to leave a message on voicemail so someone can call them later with information in their native language. School districts should check their own staff to see if there are people who can help with interpretation in cases when families arrive unexpectedly. Another option is using a trained interpreter from an over-the-phone service.

Safe and Welcoming

The pandemic and previous school shootings have resulted in new health and safety protocols. These are intended to protect staff, children, and parents. Although safety and good health are the top priorities of parents, these protocols may make it more difficult for families to come to school.

School security measures such as metal detectors and locked gates may discourage immigrant families from visiting the school (Zarate, 2007). Visitor/parent sign in policies may also be intimidating, especially if they require documentation such as a driver's license. It is incumbent upon schools to ensure that staff know how to implement safety procedures in a friendly and respectful manner and to make certain families understand the rationale behind them. These procedures should be included in family and student orientation.

Schools should not assume that staff possess the needed skills to make schools friendly. Businesses often undertake extensive training in customer relations. Schools should do the same and support all staff, including bus drivers, with the appropriate training and protocols needed to work with immigrant families.

Undocumented Families

The Urban Institute (2020) reports that one out of every four children has at least one immigrant parent. In some states, such as California, that percentage is almost half. About one third of immigrant parents are undocumented (Urban Institute, 2019). This means they do not have permission to live in the United States. These family members may have overstayed a legal visa or entered the country without permission (Sember, 2015) (Table 3.2).

Any person who is undocumented may be deported or have deportation proceedings started against them at any time. This creates a highly stressful situation for families and children who worry about their parents being deported (Ee & Gandara, 2020). Thus, school security procedures intended to keep students safe may actually heighten deportation fears for immigrant families if not handled in an appropriate manner.

Table 3.2 Various Immigrant Statuses

Immigrant	Refugees or Asylees	Temporary Protective Status	Undocumented
Immigrant is a general term that encompasses anyone who has come to another country for an extended period of time. There are many types of immigrant statuses. If immigrants have children born in the United States, the children are U.S. citizens.	Refugees and asylees leave their home countries due to war, persecution, and human rights violations. Refugees receive permission to enter the United States before arriving, and asylees seek government permission once they arrive.	Citizens of certain designated countries may be allowed to live and work in the United States temporarily because they cannot return home due to natural disasters or armed conflict. There are currently 10 countries on the list. This temporary status adds stress for families because the protection can be removed through no fault of their own.	An undocumented immigrant is someone who lacks permission to be in the United States. Some undocumented immigrants overstayed work, student, or visitor visas.

Immigrants' Legal Rights

It is imperative that school staff have a clear understanding of the legal rights that are afforded to immigrant children by the federal government in the Supreme Court Case of Plyer vs. Doe (Brennan & Supreme Court of the United States, 1981). Public schools cannot deny admission to students on the basis of undocumented status. Staff cannot ask parents or students to disclose their immigration status nor can school admission be denied based on lack of documentation such as driver's licenses and social security numbers (U.S. Department of Justice & U.S. Department of Education, 2014). The Intercultural Development Research Association (2019) has produced a one-page flyer that contains key points of immigrants' rights that may be used when reviewing the educational rights of immigrants with staff and posted in the school office area.

Sensitive Location

All parents should be assured that the schools will follow the Family Educational Rights and Privacy Act (FERPA) to protect student's confidential information (Koski, 2019). Additionally, schools may share with parents the federal government's position which views schools as a sensitive location and as such immigration officers generally will not arrest, interview, search, or surveil a person for immigration enforcement purposes while at a school, a known school bus stop, or an educational activity (U.S. Immigration and Customs Enforcement, n.d.).

Discipline Policies

Schools need to prioritize safety and health, have processes in place to prevent and deal with unsafe situations, and have fair discipline policies that are consistently enforced throughout the school program, including in the cafeteria, on the bus, in the gym, and during after-school activities. All students should be involved in programs to promote self-esteem, respect, and conflict resolution, thus helping to prevent bullying. These efforts should extend to cyberbullying. It is important that counselors are available to meet with students and families and to refer them to other community resources when necessary.

School Safety

The topic of school safety should be systematically reviewed with the school staff along with the reminder to staff to act upon parental/family concerns. Such a review can occur at the beginning of each semester. School staff should remain vigilant about being culturally sensitive to families' concerns and not dismiss them as being unfounded or unimportant. When the staff takes time to carefully listen to concerns, ask questions, and seek input on solutions to problems, trust is built and sensitivity shown. Such interest must come from all school staff, including teachers, and not be regarded as outside anyone's job responsibilities or duties. Such actions make schools welcome and inviting places.

Parent Spaces

Schools should consider creating a designated space or room on campus for parents and family members. Spaces may go by the name of parent room, parent hub, or family resource room. A dedicated space on campus signals to parents and families that they are welcome at the school. Spaces can be set up with adult-sized furnishings, coffee, a computer, and resource materials. This space provides a place for families to gather, connect with other parents, and meet school staff.

Central Falls, Rhode Island, credits their parent hub (space) for helping spur family engagement in its schools. "Though it may seem simple, the first step to building parent engagement in the lower grades was giving parents a space to be comfortable in the schools" (Martinez & Wizer-Vecchi, 2016, Providing Space and Facilitating Collaboration section, para. 19).

Schools as Community Resources

Schools can be more welcoming by serving as community resources and as a bridge between services offered in the community and at school. Schools have a number of facilities that are often underused. If a school facility is seen as a resource, limiting the use of that resource to only part of the day is wasteful. Opening up school facilities to the families of children served by the school makes better use of that resource. Four areas that schools could open to families are the library, the nurse's office, the athletic fields and gyms, and the classrooms. Opening these underused facilities after school or even during the day can make the school a community center.

Library

The school library can serve as a literacy center for the families of children in the school. School librarians should purchase books in the languages spoken by the family members and representing the cultures of families. Often, second language communities will have free newspapers in the languages spoken in the area. Having these available in the library will help family members feel comfortable in the library. If family members feel comfortable using the library, they are more likely to volunteer as book readers or shelving books.

Nurse's Office/Health Services

The nurse's office is another area that can help welcome families into the school community. The nurse can make referrals for various health services in the community, such as immunizations, dental work, eyeglasses, and mental health services. In addition, some schools have partnered with community organizations to set up health clinics at the school.

Health services are particularly important for children who live in poverty because they are more likely to suffer from physical and mental illnesses. More information about community health partnerships is available at the Center for Health and Health Care in Schools (http://healthinschools.org). This site is dedicated to helping schools and communities start school health centers. Schools also can become welcoming places to families by providing athletic facilities for the local community.

Gyms/Sports Fields

Schools often have gymnasiums, basketball courts, and playing fields that can be used by children and families after school. Families who participate in an after-school sports or recreation program are more likely to feel comfortable visiting the school with their children. Supervision of the programs can come through local Boys and Girls Clubs or the United Way. Another source of supervision can come with a city–school partnership.

Summer

Alternative summer programs are sprouting up across the country, especially to serve the needs of lower income students. In order to resolve funding and staffing problems, school districts partner with other public and private agencies and seek grants and funding available for summer programs serving low-income youth. More information on these funding sources is available from the National Summer Learning Association (https://www.summerlearning.org/).

Although these programs differ, the most successful ones combine learning with the recreational aspects of summer camp. Because of the less formal nature of the learning and the involvement in the community, families feel more welcome at these programs and are more likely to become involved. See an example of a successful summer program, Aim High, in Chapter 10.

After-School Programs

Most parents view after-school programs as a way to provide not only a safe environment for children after school but also access to a wide range of activities and enriching opportunities for children (Afterschool Alliance, 2014). After-school programs are especially important to immigrant families as they may provide after-school supervision until parents get out of work, extra assistance with schoolwork, and an opportunity to help children to foster social skills and participate in other enrichment opportunities (Bridging Refugee Youth and Children's Services, n.d.-a).

Schools should consider how to offer such activities on their campus either through existing school staff or linking with community agencies to provide programs on campus. After-school programs offered at the school site allow students easy access to participation and remove barriers to participation such as lack of transportation and cost.

Building Community

Immigrant families often do not feel a part of the school community. At the high school level, sports, especially football, bring together many members of the community. They cheer the team on, sell sodas and snacks, and see old friends. However, families from other countries may not connect with football because it is primarily an American game. Therefore, other efforts may be necessary to bring immigrant families into the school community. Schools can promote sports such as soccer, which is played around the world by both boys and girls. They can also do activities such as creating gardens, painting murals, or developing multicultural recipe books that may engage families that would not be involved in more traditional activities (see online support materials). Clubs that reflect the students' culture may also encourage students and families to become more involved in school. For example, Hispanic families may relate more to mariachi music or folklorico dancing than to traditional dance activities.

Activity: Knowing Your School Community

Purpose: Identify cultural assets within the community to support schools. This activity is based on suggestions made in the article, *A Place for All Families*, by Ramirez and Soto-Hinman (2009).

Participants: New teachers and staff

Preparation and resources: Map of the community that outlines the school attendance zone; form of transportation: walking, cars, or buses; and paper and pencil for taking notes.

Description of activity: On three different occasions throughout the school year, travel two or three miles out into the community using the school as a starting point. Take a different route each time you visit the community. Analyze what students pass each day on their way to and from school. Note the types of homes students live in, the shops and businesses located on the route, languages spoken and seen in print, medical facilities, childcare facilities, community agencies, parks or recreational opportunities, places of worship, libraries, and general landmarks and landscapes that the students pass.

After completing the community travel, teachers record observations and discuss with the faculty what they have observed and noted. The discussion should center on the assets of the community rather than a negative discussion of what the community does not have. Questions may arise from the debriefing/discussion sessions. They may be collected and posed to parents and community members. School staff should be encouraged to examine stereotypes they may have held about their communities prior to the community trips.

Community trip discussions may be extended to a brainstorming session about how the community can be better utilized to engage all families. Such ideas may include exploring the potential of contacting places of worship and local businesses to be community partners to help communicate school events and information. For example, a local hair or nail salon could have copies of the school newsletter available for families to read in their native language. Copies of children's books in native languages might also be available for children to read and look at while children wait for family members. Local grocery stores may have fliers in students' native language advertising weekly specials. Such fliers may be utilized in a family literacy activity that teaches concepts about print.

Options: A variation on this activity would be to include all school personnel, including veteran teachers, bus drivers, cafeteria workers, office staff, paraprofessionals, and security guards on community trips and the resulting discussions of community assets that can be used to support the school.

Activity: Mystery Shopper

Purpose: This activity allows your school to measure the quality of the experience for first-time visitors to the school. Do the visitors have a warm and welcoming experience?

One of the great inventions of the fast-food world is the Mystery Shopper. The Mystery Shopper is someone who is paid to visit a restaurant at different times of the day to find out about the dining experience. They are employed by the owner or manager to find out how the customer sees the store. Is the store clean? Was the service polite and efficient? Was the food good? Try this at your own school by finding someone who has never been to your school before and asking them to visit.

Participants: A school administrator invites someone to come to the school posing as the parent of a child new to the neighborhood or as someone interested in volunteering at the school. It is best if the person is from a cultural group that is prevalent in the local community.

Preparation and resources: Hire someone as a *Mystery Shopper* and decide what they should look for. As few people as possible should know about this project in advance because you want to get an honest assessment of the school climate.

Description of activity: The *Mystery Shopper* may look at different things on different campuses, but the following are some suggestions:

◆ Is signage clear and in the languages of the school community?
◆ How hard is it to navigate security?
◆ How hard is it to find the office?
◆ Are there bilingual/multilingual staff available in the office?
◆ How are visitors greeted when they come to the office?
◆ How are families greeted when students are brought to the school campus?
◆ Do school staff members greet students and families by name?
◆ What is posted on the walls of the school? Are there student work displays and lists of upcoming school and community events?
◆ What interactions occur between teachers and parents or family members?
◆ Does the school treat parents who do not speak English differently from English-speaking parents?

Share the findings with all stakeholders and discuss areas of strength and areas needing improvement.

Options: Have different *Mystery Shoppers* and compare how the school treats parents who speak English and those who don't; how men are treated compared to women; how professionally dressed people are treated compared to people dressed for manual labor; how people in nonwestern traditional garb are treated compared to someone who shows up in western dress.

Another potential Mystery Shopper activity is to have a parent or family member try to schedule a meeting with a faculty member or an administrator.

Activity: School Safety Survey

Purpose: School safety is a high priority for all families. Educators are often not aware of the perceptions of the school in the community. Although the school itself may appear safe, walking to and from school or taking the bus may present security problems. That is why it is important to find out the perceptions of school safety from all those involved, including culturally and linguistically diverse families.

Participants: Families

Preparation and resources: Plans to gather information. Written surveys in the languages spoken by the families in the community may be a starting point but additional meetings out in the community may be necessary to gather information from diverse families. Prepare responses to concerns that are raised during this process.

Description of activity: questions will vary from campus to campus, but suggestions include:

◆ Does your child feel safe in school? If not, when does your child feel he or she is in danger? (For example, some students feel secure in class but are taunted on the playground.)
◆ Does your child feel safe going to and from school? If not, what makes your child feel insecure?
◆ Is your child bullied at school? If so, when?
◆ Do you have concerns about your child's health at school?
◆ Have you ever contacted the school about a health or safety concern? What was that concern? How was it handled?

After information has been collected, it should be reviewed, and plans made to address concerns. Family members should be informed of the steps being taken. Follow-up to the surveys is essential even if changes can't be made quickly.

Options: Staff members may want to discuss topics related to safety at a meeting. The staff might consider questions like these:

◆ Do you feel safe at the school? If not, what concerns you?
◆ Is there a school climate or safety committee?
◆ Are families and community members a part of the committee?
◆ What does this committee do and how often does it meet?
◆ What process is used when family members have safety concerns? How long does this take?
◆ How and in what languages are school safety measures communicated to families?
◆ What changes have been made at your campus based on community or family input related to safety issues?

Relevant Literature

The Girl Who Smiled Beads: A Story of War and What Comes After by Clemantine Wamariya and Elizabeth Weil (2018) chronicles Clemantine's true story of escape from Rwanda during the 1994 massacre when she was six. Clemantine and her 15-year-old sister survived refugee camps, danger, and hunger through seven African countries over a six-year period. When Clementine was 12, she was granted refugee status in the United States and was sponsored by a family in the suburbs while her sister, now a single mother, struggled to survive in Chicago nearby. Eventually, their parents were found and came to live with her sister. Clemantine relates not only the events of her life through age 30 but her constant trauma from her early years and her struggles to become her own person. *Chapter book.*

A Step from Heaven, by An Na (2003), describes the life of a girl, Young Ju, who is born in Korea and who moves to the United States with her family as a young girl. As she gets older, she learns more about the struggles of her family in adapting to American culture, which does not have the same values as her parents. As Young Ju grows older, she begins to adapt to American ways, which upsets her family. Eventually, the stress of living in the United States becomes too much for her father, and he returns to Korea. Young Ju is left alone in the United States with her mother. The story challenges the stereotype that families from Asian descent easily assimilate in the United States and become successful yet affirms that people can be resilient when making choices between two cultures. *Chapter book.*

References

Afterschool Alliance. (2014). *America after 3 pm: Afterschool programs in demand.* https://www.org/documents/AA3PM-2014/AA3PM_Key_Findings.pdf

Brennan, W. J. & Supreme Court of the United States. (1981). *U.S. reports: Plyer v. Doe, 457 U.S. 202.* [Periodical] Retrieved from the Library of Congress, https://www.loc.gov/item/usrep457202/

Bridging Refugee Youth and Children's Services. (n.d.-a). *Promising practices in after-school programming for refugee youth and children.* https://brycs.org/youth-development/promising-practices-in-after-school-programming-for-refugee-youth-and-children/

Bridging Refugees and Youth and Children's Services. (n.d.-b). *Welcoming and orienting newcomer students to U.S. schools.* https://brycs.org/schools/welcoming-and-orienting-newcomer-students-to-u-s-schools/

Crawford Elementary School. (n.d.). *Refugee welcome booklet.* https://crawford. aurorak12.org/community/refugee-support/

Ee, J. & Gandara, P. (2020). The impact of immigration enforcement on the nation's schools. *American Educational Research Journal*, 57(2), 840–871. https://journals.sagepub.com/doi/pdf/10.3102/0002831219862998

English Learner Portal. (2019, August 12). *Orienting English learners & immigrant families to schools.* [Video] YouTube. https://www.youtube.com/watch?v=YXMYPY-B0d8&feature=youtu.be

English Learner Portal. (n.d.). *Resource checklist orienting English learners and immigrant families.* https://www.englishlearnerportal.com/checklist-orientation

Houston Independent School District. (n.d.). *Welcoming walkthrough overview.* https://www.houstonisd.org/site/handlers/filedownload.ashx?moduleinstanceid=180683&dataid=140776&FileName=Welcoming-School-Walk-Through-Guide-3.pdf

Ikhar, A. (2018). *Somali-English bilingualism: Somali parents' beliefs and strategies for raising bilingual children* (master's thesis). St. Cloud State University. https://repository.stcloudstate.edu/cgi/viewcontent.cgi?article=1187&context=engl_etds

Intercultural Development Research Association. (2019). *Welcoming immigrant students in school.* https://www.idra.org/wp-content/uploads/2019/08/Welcoming-Immigrant-Students-IDRA-Infographic-2019-Letter-Bilingual-sm.pdf

Kentucky Department of Education. (n.d.). *Family and community engagement.* https://education.ky.gov/districts/SBDM/Documents/Family%20Community%20Engagement%20Participant%27s%20Guide.pdf

Koski, W. S. (2019, July 19). Advice on keeping immigrant students safe at school. *Stanford Law School Blog.* https://law.stanford.edu/2019/07/19/advice-on-keeping-immigrant-students-safe-at-school/

Martinez, P. & Wizer-Vecchi, J. (2016). Fostering family engagement through shared leadership in the district, schools and community. *Voices in Urban Education.* http://vue.annenberginstitute.org/issues/44/fostering-family-engagement-through-shared-leadership-district-schools-and-community

Nesloney, T. (2020). *Family engagement: How to build relationships by tearing down walls.* [Webinar] Livingtree. https://try.livingtree.com/webinar-recording/how-to-build-relationships-by-tearing-down-walls/

New York City Department of Education. (n.d.). *NYC public schools speak your language.* https://www.schools.nyc.gov/school-life/school-environment/hello

Portland Public Schools. (n.d.). *Helping multilingual families register for school.* https://mlc.portlandschools.org/programs/family_welcome_center

Ramirez, A. Y. & Soto-Hinman, I. (2009). A place for all families. *Educational Leadership*, 66(7), 79–82.

Sember, B. (2015, April). Who is an undocumented immigrant? *Legal Zoom.* https://www.legalzoom.com/articles/who-is-an-undocumented-immigrant

Short, D. J. & Boyson, B. A. (2012). *Helping newcomer students succeed in secondary schools and beyond.* Center for Applied Linguistics. https://www.cal.org/resource-center/publications-products/helping-newcomer-students

Underhill. J. (2014, January 22). Is your school parent-friendly? *PTO Today.* https://www.ptotoday.com/pto-today-articles/article/398-is-your-school-parent-friendly

Urban Institute. (2019, March 14). *Part of us: A data-driven look at children of immigrants.* https://www.urban.org/features/part-us-data-driven-look-children-immigrants

Urban Institute. (2020). *Visualizing trends for children of immigrants.* http://apps.urban.org/features/children-of-immigrants/

U.S. Department of Education. (2017). *Newcomer toolkit.* https://www2.ed.gov/about/offices/list/oela/newcomers-toolkit/ncomertoolkit.pdf

U.S. Department of Justice & U.S. Department of Education. (2014, May 8). *Dear colleague letter: School enrollment procedures.* https://www2.ed.gov/about/offices/list/ocr/letters/colleague-201405.pdf

U.S. Department of Justice & U.S. Department of Education. (2015). *Information for limited English proficient (LEP) parents and guardians and for schools and school districts that communicate with them.* https://www2.ed.gov/about/offices/list/ocr/docs/dcl-factsheet-lep-parents-201501.pdf

U.S. Immigration and Customs Enforcement. (n.d.). FAQ on sensitive locations and courthouse arrests. Retrieved January 2, 2021, from https://www.ice.gov/ero/enforcement/sensitive-loc

Warsi, S. (2017). Welcoming refugee children into early childhood classrooms. *Teaching Young Children*, 10(5). https://www.naeyc.org/resources/pubs/tyc/aug2017/welcoming-refugee-children-into-classrooms

Zarate, M. E. (2007). *Understanding Latino parental involvement in education: Perceptions, expectations, and recommendations.* (ED502065). ERIC. https://files.eric.ed.gov/fulltext/ED502065.pdf

4

Communicating with Immigrant Families

Scenario: Summer Contact

During the summer, Ms. Driscoll, an elementary school teacher, was given a list of her students for the following year and asked to contact them before the start of the year. She had questions to ask each family. She had spent most of the morning and had only reached one family, but she needed to schedule a Somali interpreter to complete that questionnaire. Finally, she reached the mother of Lizzy Cavazos, who spoke English. She introduced herself and began down the list of questions, including family housing and food needs, internet availability, and the number and ages of children in the household. Everything seemed to be fine with this family. At last, she had finished one questionnaire.

The social worker called Ms. Driscoll the very next day and confirmed that she had Lizzy Cavazos in her class. The social worker had met Lizzy, who she already knew, at the location where they were handing out lunches to students who qualified for free lunches over the summer. After talking to Lizzy for a few minutes, she asked her how she and her family were doing. Lizzy told her the free lunch was the only meal she received each day. Her father had lost his job, and her mother needed to stay home to take care of the baby. Lizzy's mother seemed friendly and happy to hear from Lizzy's future teacher, but she had not mentioned any of these problems to Ms. Driscoll.

Building Relationships

Many educators, like Ms. Driscoll in the scenario above, are anxious to gain information from families, but they only will be marginally successful unless they develop relationships and trust first. While U.S. culture tends to be task centered, other cultures around the world emphasize relationships (Elliott et al., 2016a). Real relationships and trust take time to develop, but Ms. Driscoll might have been more successful if she had begun with some information about herself and her goals for Lizzy in her class. Then, she might have asked Lizzy's mother about her hopes for Lizzy. Relationships are best established around teachers' and families' shared interest in student success. Ms. Driscoll could then move on to things like, "I would really like to keep in touch with you throughout the school year. How could I best do that? Would a free hotspot for the internet be useful for your family to stay in touch with the school?" This conversation indicates an interest in Lizzy and developing a relationship with Lizzy's family throughout the school year.

"For many educators, the shift is not to communicate more but to communicate strategically. By centering (on) relationships and family well-being, educators can tap into parents' existing motivation to help their children succeed" (Brady et al., 2020, p. 5).

A report on working with minority families makes five recommendations for building relationships with minority families:

- ◆ Embrace parents as a critical component to student success;
- ◆ Understand that the parent is the child's first teacher;
- ◆ Believe in, promote, and implement two-way communication where schools communicate with parents and parents communicate with school officials;
- ◆ Discuss values and develop an understanding of how experiences of racism and classism play out in a school setting and affect communication and interaction; and
- ◆ Ask questions and listen to how parents feel disconnected from the schools. Do more listening than talking (Mexican American Legal Defense and Educational Fund & National Education Association, 2010, p. 27).

Working with both pre-service and practicing teachers, we have often heard about bad experiences with families of school-aged children or about families who never communicate with the school. However, when these teachers worked with families one-on-one, their attitudes shifted dramatically. In one program, we introduced future teachers to children and families through an after-school tutoring program. We had our students work with an individual child on developing literacy skills. The students also had to have two-way communication with the family members who brought the child to the program through informal discussions and formal conferencing. While reflecting with our future teacher candidates, we were amazed at how much they were learning through this communication with the families. Although all of our students were preparing to teach in either bilingual or English as a second language settings, they felt their communication skills with the families were complicated. Explaining academic terminology to family members who were not up on the latest academic jargon was difficult. And it was difficult for bilingual students to find an adequate translation for words learned only in English.

Our students also realized that their teacher preparation program had not prepared them to work with families. They had been placed in classrooms for observations, but few had previous opportunities to actually communicate one-on-one with a family member. Finally, because our students had to work so closely with family members, they began to feel a great deal more empathy and respect for them. One day, the roads flooded and many of the tutors and professors had a hard time reaching the school and wondered if any of the families would show up. But the families literally rolled up their pants and walked through the water to make sure their children got to the tutoring session. Seen from a distance, the families often seemed intimidating or uninterested in their children's education. When met face to face with the child's best interest at heart, they found that families were deeply involved and committed to their children's success in school.

Language

Educators and families both say that language is one of the greatest obstacles to creating reciprocal relationships between immigrant families and schools. Surveys should be conducted with all families in the school to determine what specific languages families understand and speak (see Chapter 2).

Table 4.1 Interpretation and Translation

Interpretation	Translation
The oral rendering of one language into another. This includes sign language.	The written rendering of one language into another language.

Sometimes, it may not be enough to know what general language they speak. For example, Spanish interpretation for families from Honduras will differ from families from Cuba. There are three distinct forms of Persian: Farsi, Dari, and Tajiki, which is important to know when contacting an interpreter. Educators sometimes assume that the family members of a student who speaks English fluently will also speak English well. However, family members may not have had the same educational opportunities in English as the student and may not speak English fluently.

Interpretation Law

The law requires that any information or services that are available to English-speaking families also be available to other families in languages they understand (Table 4.1). This includes websites and other online platforms. The public schools also must use professional interpreters rather than family members or untrained staff members. Although interpretation has been required since the 1964 Civil Rights Act, the specifics were made clear in 2015 (The U.S. Department of Justice & U.S. Department of Education, 2015).

Interpretation Effectiveness

Gardner of Immigrant Connections (2020b) has created a continuum for interpretation (Figure 4.1).

The best alternative is a professionally trained interpreter who does face-to-face interpretation. The cons to this are that it usually takes time to

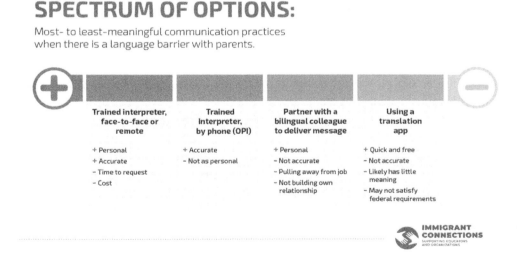

Figure 4.1 Spectrum of Interpretation Options (Gardner, 2020b).

schedule a professional face-to-face interpreter and there are greater costs. Large districts may have professional interpreters on the staff for common languages, but this alternative is often not possible for smaller districts or languages that are only spoken by a few families in the district. The Family Educational Rights Privacy Act (n.d.), otherwise known as FERPA, sets out guidance for schools on how to ensure children's and families' privacy in educational settings. Having a family member, friend, or neighbor act as an interpreter can violate the guidance on family privacy as well as the Civil Rights Act mentioned above.

The second-best alternative is a trained interpreter who works through video conferencing or phone either with teachers and family members who are together at school or with them on their own devices in different locations. There are various services, such as LanguageLine and Language Link, that can be placed on contract for this purpose. This is not as personal as face-to-face interpretation but can be effective if everyone cannot be together in one place.

The third alternative, which is often used by schools due to cost and convenience, is having a bilingual staff member serve as an interpreter. It is important that when this occurs, the teacher also is present so he can build a relationship with the family. Disadvantages to this approach are the interpreter is often pulled away from his regular job and may lack impartiality. Bilingual staff members with dual roles may become overly attached or involved with the families, leading to a conflict of interest.

The fourth alternative is using a translation app. Talking Points, for example, allows the teachers to text parents in English and the parent receives the text in their preferred language automatically. The parents can then text back in their home language and the teacher receives the message in English. Breiseth (2020) warns that these translation apps are not a substitute for professional interpreters who understand the community, education terms, and can help build relationships with immigrant families.

A child or sibling could be used to set up a later meeting with a professional interpreter but should never be used for longer communication. The authors have learned through their own mistakes that a good interpreter is much more than someone who speaks the family's language. Although people may speak a language well enough for daily interactions, they may lack the technical language in English or the other language to interpret educational issues. People who speak a language fluently don't always write fluently and care must be taken that letters that go home are professionally done, as families may wonder about the school's competency if a letter is filled with errors in their native language. Lynch and Hanson (2004) say that effective interpreters and translators are proficient in the dialect of the family, understand cross-cultural communication, and understand the content that needs to be conveyed to the families.

Recruiting and Training Interpreters

Due to the lack of professional interpreters in many regions of the country and in less common languages, schools are looking to their local community. They may partner with organizations that serve immigrants in their community or train multilingual people in the community to be educational interpreters. The Syracuse City School District is doing both as well as using a professional service that provides interpretation over the phone. With thousands of emergent bilingual students and 72 languages spoken, they had to get creative. They have hired and trained community members, called Nationality Workers, who interpret for families in Somali, Swahili, Mai-Mai, Nepali, Pashto, Urdu, Burmese, Karen, and Arabic. Nationality Workers help with school enrollment, informational sessions, and parent–teacher conferences to name a few of their roles. In addition, the school district hires contract interpreters through Interfaith Works of Central New York. The school district explains that interpretation with families is important both because it is the law and because it is essential to student success (Mathewson, 2016).

The National Accreditation of Educational Translators and Interpreters of Spoken Language (NAETISL, https://www.naetisl.net/) was formed to assist school districts understand the standards, qualifications, and accreditation requirements for educational translators and interpreters with the goal of enhancing family engagement, student achievement, and meaningful home–school connection according to Chairperson Ana Soler (personal communication, September 9, 2020). For financial reasons, most districts hire people who are bilingual to work in multiple capacities, including interpretation. She says districts should begin by testing the language proficiency of the employees, using a service such as Language Testing International, rather than depending on self-reports of abilities. If interpreters do not do well, districts can assist them with training and use them for non-critical situations until their skills improve. Other school staff such as secretaries, cafeteria workers, or bus drivers who have bilingual skills also could be trained as interpreters.

In addition to being truly bilingual or multilingual, ongoing professional development is crucial according to Soler. Many interpreter programs are surfacing now, especially online. NAETISL is developing criteria that school districts can use to evaluate the courses to make sure they provide the curriculum needed to support families and schools effectively. Soler emphasizes that the difficulty of tasks vary, and the skills of the interpreter must match the situation. For example, interpreting evaluations and special education in-formation is difficult because of the specialized language and the impact it may have on the rest of the student's life. Simultaneous interpretation, which occurs when someone is speaking and people are listening to an interpreter through headphones, is also very difficult. On the other hand, taking people on a tour of the school in the families' home language may not be as challeng-ing. In order to respond to these issues, Washoe County Schools in Nevada developed a tier system for interpreters so they can better match them with specific tasks.

Educators Preparing to Work with Interpreters

Just as interpreters need special training to work in a school setting, educa-tors need to learn to work with interpreters. In face-to-face settings, the edu-cator should always look at the family members, not the interpreter. In both face-to-face and virtual settings, leave time for the family to ask questions and for the interpreter to translate to English. If there seems to be a misun-derstanding, try restating the idea using different terms. It is often difficult to make a direct translation between two languages. For example, English has over 171,000 words in current use compared to about 93,000 for Spanish and about 86,000 for Mandarin.

Weinzapfel (2020) explains that simplifying improves communication in any language. She says you should not "dumb-down" messages, but you should make them understandable. For example, "post-secondary" can be re-placed with "after high-school" or "assessment" can be replaced with "test." These phrases are easier to understand in English as well as easier to trans-late. Weinzapfel also says educators need to be careful not to overwhelm fam-ilies with too many messages or messages that are too long. She says to parcel out information in shorter communications, each with two or three important points.

Using Graphs to Communicate

Some schools and districts use the universal language of graphs to enhance communication with immigrant families. Most families, including immigrant families, have some idea of how their child is doing in school but don't know how that compares with other children at that grade level or the academic goals for the year. The Academic Parent–Teacher Teams use bar graphs to provide that information to immigrant families (Adams, 2016). They show beginning levels in math and reading and current levels, so families can see progress. Then, they show average levels for students at that grade level and the academic goals for the year. Some families may feel discouraged, but the program, which is used in over 300 schools, explains to families what they can do at home to help their children even if they don't have a formal education or English skills. Every family can help their child learn.

Culture and Expectations

The Nationality Workers in Syracuse not only do interpretation, they also bridge cultural gaps. For example, families from many other cultures may not be familiar with the expectations of parent–teacher conferences. Syracuse holds sessions in English with newcomer families grouped by languages and an appropriate interpreter with each group. After the English-speaking facilitator says a few sentences, each interpreter repeats the information for their language group so the immigrant families can better understand the expectations of U.S. schools. Other school procedures that may be different for immigrant families are grading systems, standardized testing, various language assistance classes, special needs support, and checking students out of school early.

When we think of culture, we usually think of things such as food, clothing, and music, but according to Elliott et al. (2016b), less visible differences are the "trust and respect" breakers (p. 2). Elliott et al. (2016a) have created a chart for cross-cultural communication. The chart contains generalizations that may not be true for everyone within the culture but provide guidance for differences that may occur. Cultures vary in the space between people during an in-person conversation, turn-taking, and how time is treated. All of these factors may impact the communication between schools and families. For example, a teacher may have a conference with a family member. The teacher may come from a culture in which people take turns speaking and allow the other person to complete their thought before interjecting an idea. The family member may come from a culture in which several people speak at once. The teacher may find the family member rude because he keeps interrupting, and the family member may believe the teacher is not interested in his ideas. Sometimes, there are also differing views of time. A teacher may schedule several conferences or phone calls one right after another. A family member, who believes that one spends as much time on a task as necessary to complete it, may find it disconcerting when the conference is ended before all pertinent issues have been discussed.

Virtual Communication

Virtual communication allows teachers to continue to build relationships with families when they cannot come to the school for any number of reasons, including a pandemic, bad weather, lack of transportation, or lack of child-care. Schools and families need to be aware of the importance of keeping current contact information. Immigrant families often move to find work. If they use prepaid cell phones, their phone numbers may change frequently too. Use emergency numbers, other families in the neighborhood, and community and faith-based organizations to track down the families if necessary. For example, one 19,000 student district along the Texas–Mexico border lost touch with about 1,000 students during the pandemic. It is also important that families know how to contact the school (Breiseth, 2020).

Once you make contact with the family, find out what methods of communication are preferred by families and try to use them at least to begin the process. Some families prefer phone calls, others like texting, and still others prefer messaging through social media, such as Facebook. This information could be learned through a beginning of the year family survey or a telephone call to the family. Various cultures tend to prefer different apps. For example, the Chinese often use WeChat, South Koreans like Kakao Talk, and Latin Americans tend to prefer WhatsApp. Once you discover what families prefer to use, you can develop a text group for families who prefer the same app and use it for messages that need to reach all families in the group (Gardner, 2020a).

In addition to knowing how families prefer to communicate, it is also important to know when they can communicate (Breiseth, 2020). One phone may be shared among several family members who cannot return calls or texts during work. Cultural norms concerning who in the family communicates with the school are also important. Make sure family members have your phone number and the phone number of any interpreters that may be used because the family may not respond to calls or texts from an unknown source.

A number of schools have formed social media groups for specific members of their community. An example is: The Karen Family Facebook Group in Roseville, Minnesota. Information is posted in English and Karen, a language spoken in Myanmar. Although this is a public group that can be viewed by anyone, it is possible to make these groups private for members only to protect the privacy of immigrant families.

Digital Availability and Knowledge

Some school districts may be requiring teachers to use specific communication tools, which makes it difficult for some families and teachers. Millions of Americans, mostly living in rural areas, lack access to internet coverage, and millions more have access to broadband internet, but can't afford it. Vogels et al. conducted a poll in April 2020 of families whose children were learning at home due to coronavirus school closures. About 22 percent of all families said they lacked reliable internet and 43 percent of low-income families reported their only internet was on the cell phone.

Not only do families need a device and internet to successfully communicate with schools, they also need knowledge of specific online platforms that may be used by the school, such as Class Dojo, Google Classroom, Seesaw, or Zoom. If it is possible, conduct in-school sessions in which families bring the devices they use at home, be it a tablet, computer, or phone (see the *Technology for Families Activity* in Chapter 5). One school district even set up sessions at a drive-in theater, where families brought their devices, and instructions with photos were displayed on the screen. Each family had a red card in their vehicle to indicate they needed help from the technology specialists walking around the parking lot.

One real school that we will call Sample School here posted grades on a special portal to keep the grades confidential. This system allowed families to see grades throughout the semester, not just at report card time. All the information was in English and Spanish, the first language of many immigrants in the district. Some of the educators at the school couldn't understand why some immigrant families were not taking advantage of this system or why they hadn't called for a conference if their child was getting low grades. The school had not considered their system from the families' point of view. First, families needed to know that the portal existed. The information about the portal was on the school webpage. If families did not have internet, they wouldn't have seen the information about the portal, and even if they saw it, it might not make sense to them. Next, families needed to come to the school office during business hours to get a password for the student portal. Due to work, transportation, and other issues that would be extremely difficult for many families. Then, the family would need to be technology savvy to get into the portal, and finally, they would need to understand the grading system, which might be different from their origin country. Even if the family made it through all these hurdles, their cultural background might keep them from calling the school and questioning the teacher about the grades. Rather than assuming families are not interested in their children's success, it is important to consider what cultural, knowledge, and technology assumptions may be keeping them from being engaged with the school (see *Evaluating School-Home Communication Activity* in this chapter).

Telephone Communication

The telephone also may be a simple tool for on-going communication with immigrant families. During a webinar, Reider (2020) of English Learner Portal asked teachers how they were keeping in touch with families of ELs during the pandemic, the overwhelming response was "by telephone." One teacher was asked how she had over 90 percent family participation even during the pandemic and she replied, "Oh, I talked to them on the phone all the time before the pandemic." With all the new apps and online platforms, sometimes educators forget about the power of a one-on-one telephone call. While some families lack computers and high-speed internet, almost all of them have cell phones (Pew Research Center, 2019). Phone calls show families the teacher cares about the student and family (see *Telephone Communication Activity*).

Parent–Teacher Conferences

Parent–teacher conferences, especially face-to-face, offer a great opportunity to develop relationships and trust, but they also can be full of cultural and language pitfalls. Try to schedule conferences on different days and at different times to accommodate families' schedules. Make sure that you have privacy and enough time for the conference. In advance, find out if the person coming to the conference speaks English or another language you speak. If there is no common language, arrange to have an appropriate interpreter there. Conferences are a good time to get to know the family and child better as well as share student progress and expectations. Teachers may also ask what other services they would like the school to provide. For example, parents at one school requested evening English classes. Even if the school was unable to provide this service, they might be able to partner with a community organization that could.

Ask what the student enjoys about school and if the student has mentioned any concerns about school to the family. If possible, share the student's work samples with the family so they can see what the student is doing in class. If there are any concerns about the work, it is easier to show the family rather than just tell them about it. When it is necessary to use educational jargon, make sure to explain the terminology. For example, "your child had some trouble with the *fluency* portion of the test that measures how quickly a student reads and how many errors he makes." End with an upbeat message and try to give the family something to take home. There are some websites online that provide handouts in a variety of languages. For example, the ¡Colorín Colorado! (n.d.) website is a free multilingual site for families and educators. Reading tip sheets for parents of babies through third grade are available in 13 languages.

It is especially important to be aware of cultural differences that might cause misunderstandings during the discussion (Elliott et al., 2016a). For example, in general, people from Asian or Latino backgrounds are less direct in both their questions and their answers than African and Anglo people. Forest Grove, Oregon, has created an educators' cultural toolkit, partially to improve communication with families (Brady et al., 2020). They have found that *good* communication with minority and low-income families focuses on the family rather than the individual child or adult. They suggest asking "How is your family doing?" rather than "How are you doing?" (Brady et al., p. 4). Another cultural difference is taking notes during a conference. People from the United States often view it as a way to remember what was said, but people from other countries may have had negative experiences when people asked them questions and took notes. Therefore, it is probably best to jot down notes after the family has left.

Community Outreach

Home Visits

Some schools encourage teachers to go out to each students' home in pairs and other programs, such as Head Start, require home visits. In the Parent Teacher Home Visit Project, educators make two family visits a year in the home or a nearby location, such as a park. The visits are always voluntary for educators and families and arranged in advance. Teachers are trained and compensated for visits outside their school day. The focus of the first visit is relationship-building and the second one is aimed at academic success. Teachers reach out to families across the spectrum, so there is no stigma. Educators conduct visits in pairs and reflect afterward. Research on the program shows that it improves student attendance and academic success and teachers' capacity to collaborate with families (Sheldon & Jung, 2015). Stories from families, teachers, and administrators indicate that it makes a real difference in the relationships between families and the school.

For safety and privacy reasons, some school districts have replaced home visits, which are more personal, with visits to community centers, local churches, or other locations where many people from the community gather. This is especially important for immigrant families, who may not feel comfortable at school or may not have transportation to get to school. Clergymen and other community leaders can serve as liaisons between the school and immigrant families who have children at the school.

Families to Families

Most families gain a great deal of information about school from other families. This is especially true of immigrant families, who are much more likely to contact someone who speaks their language than call the school and struggle to communicate. Unfortunately, this information is not always accurate. The school can still take advantage of this method of communication by enlisting family members from various language and cultural backgrounds and providing them with accurate information. Recruit volunteers who have had children at your school for at least a year and are willing to help contact other families. Try to get as many volunteers who speak a language other than English as possible. Then, provide these volunteers with important information that the school would like to be communicated to families, such as school hours, grading systems, required immunizations, upcoming meetings, and homework policies. Provide them with the information in writing in the languages that they will be using and make sure that both the volunteers and the families they contact have names, telephone numbers, and emails of people who can provide answers to their questions. Then, ask the volunteers to contact other families in their neighborhood. If they are not comfortable going door to door, they can contact people at other local meeting places, including grocery stores, churches, and parks. One of the authors remembers getting some of the best information about her children's elementary school from other families whose children were playing at the local park.

Activity: Difficult Communication Practice Scenarios

Purpose: Most of the time educators have to respond to difficult communication on the spot, but this activity allows educators to think more deeply about how they would respond to difficult situations and reflect with other educators about different ways to handle these challenging conversations.

Participants: Teachers and administrators

Preparation and resources: Prepare copies of the different scenarios for the group to discuss.

Description of activity: Teachers and administrators will discuss the following scenarios and questions in small groups. After they discuss how each situation could be handled better, they can discuss the possible solutions with the whole group. These are real scenarios, and there is no one correct answer or simple solution.

◆ **Scenario 1.** Ms. Tan has sent three notes home with Raul, an emergent bilingual, asking that his mother call or come to school to discuss his academic progress. After three weeks, she has received no response by phone, in writing, or in person.
1   What could be the reasons for a lack of response?
2   What should Ms. Tan do now in order to speak to one of Raul's family members?

◆ **Scenario 2.** Mr. Lopez has a conference with Mr. Sanchez, the father of Sergio, who has been involved in several fights at school with Ramiro. When Mr. Lopez asks for Mr. Sanchez's help to stop the fighting, Mr. Sanchez claims that Ramiro has been bullying Sergio, and he told Sergio to stand up for himself and fight back. Mr. Sanchez asks Mr. Lopez, "Do you just want him to stand there and get beat up? I have complained about Ramiro picking on Sergio on the bus and nothing has been done."

1   What should Mr. Lopez say to Mr. Sanchez now?
2   What can Mr. Lopez and others do to stop the fighting?
3   What types of policies and procedures might prevent similar problems with other students in the future?

◆ **Scenario 3.** Ms. Walton speaks to the mother of Meira, who is from Bosnia. Meira has been daydreaming and not completing her work at school. Through an interpreter, Ms. Walton asks the mother to talk to Meira about the problem. The next day, Ms. Walton asks Meira if her parents talked to her, and Meira says, "No, they just spanked me for not getting my schoolwork done."

1   What should Ms. Walton say to Meira?
2   What might be a more effective way to deal with children who are not completing their schoolwork?

◆ **Scenario 4.** Victor has been talking back to the teacher and being disrespectful. Ms. Garcia decides to call in his mother, Ms. Villarreal, who is a young single mother from the Dominican Republic. When Ms. Garcia explains the problem at school, Ms. Villarreal says she has the same problems at home and doesn't know what to do about it. She says, "He just doesn't want to listen to me. Can you help me?"

1   What suggestions should Ms. Garcia make to Ms. Villarreal?
2   What resources are available at your school or in your community that might help family members who are having trouble disciplining their children?

◆ **Scenario 5.** Linda doesn't hand in her homework. After numerous tries, Linda's teacher, Ms. Maupin, reaches Linda's father by phone. Although his English is not fluent, they are able to communicate. Her father says that he works at night and that Linda and five of her cousins stay with her grandmother. The grandmother is busy taking care of babies, making meals, cleaning up, and getting children to bed. She doesn't have time to supervise Linda's homework, and Linda does not have a quiet place to get it done.

1   What should Ms. Maupin say to Linda's father?
2   Do the homework policies at your school take into account families like Linda's?

Activity: Evaluating School–Home Communication

Purpose: This activity is designed to help faculty and administrators carefully examine written communication that is posted or sent home to families. It asks faculty and administrators to think about what background knowledge is necessary to understand the communication and what resources may be necessary to carry out any instructions that are included in the communication.

Participants: School faculty and administrators

Preparation and resources: Prepare for a faculty meeting. Be prepared to share the Sample School example from above. Find examples of online and/or paper notices for families from your school. Be prepared to project online or paper notices.

Description of activity: Review the Sample School example from above. Identify a piece of school correspondence that has been posted or sent to school families on a previous occasion. Ask the group:

- ◆ What knowledge and resources are needed to see a post, message, or email online?
- ◆ Is the message available in a language the family understands or does the website have a translation function?
- ◆ What background knowledge or cultural knowledge is needed to understand the message?
- ◆ If the letter or post asks the families to do something, what knowledge or resources are necessary to follow through on that information?
- ◆ Does the message use educational jargon or acronyms?
- ◆ Is the message limited to two or three important points?

Options: Extend the discussion by selecting various cultural and linguistic groups within the school community and asking how the communication could be modified and adapted to ensure that parents have a full understanding of what it is they are expected to do. Parents and community members could offer input as to what technology was needed to access the information and what background information and cultural knowledge was needed to make sense of the selected correspondence. Ask bilingual families to evaluate the quality of the translations they receive. Parent and community perceptions should be compared to the school faculty's perceptions. How similar or different were the responses? What changes are needed by the school to better communicate with immigrant families?

Do a similar activity with a grade level or subject area. Sample correspondence may include notes about parent–teacher conferences, field trips, parent–teacher organizations, fundraising, science fairs, etc.

Activity: Telephone Communication

Purpose: Telephone conversations can provide on-going communication between teachers and families and show families that teachers care about their children. Telephone calls also empower families by giving them an opportunity to express their ideas or concerns. Teachers can provide families with resource ideas specific to their needs or interests.

Participants: Teachers, families, interpreter as necessary

Preparation and resources: Teachers need to find out if families would like to be called and what times are convenient for telephone calls. Teachers may want to discuss possible questions and resources in advance.

Description of activity: Call the family at one of their designated times. Introduce yourself and tell them you just wanted to say hello and find out how their child is doing. Make it clear that you are not calling about a problem. Ask open-ended questions that allow them to express their opinions. Some ideas might be: What does your child like to do during free time at home? How is your child responding to a new program at school? Have there been any changes since last time we talked? What would you like me to know about your child? How can we support your child better at school? Take brief notes during the phone call and refer to them the next time you speak to the same family, so you can follow up on any concerns. The teacher also may want to share the names of organizations, websites, or phone numbers where the family can find useful information in their home language.

Options: When students have more than one teacher, educators can share information with the family's permission. This may also apply to family issues that would be relevant to the siblings' teachers. Teachers can work together on questions that are useful without putting the family on the spot.

Relevant Literature

My Diary from Here to There, by Amada Irma Perez (2009), describes the trip a young girl and her family take from Ciudad Juárez in Mexico to California. The protagonist of the story keeps a diary about the experiences she has driving to Tijuana and then waiting there with family until the family's green cards are issued so they can cross to the United States. Most immigrants come to the United States with documentation. *Picture book.*

Side by Side: Lado a Lado, by Monica Brown (2009), describes the story of Dolores Huerta who worked closely with Cesar Chavez through the development of the United Farm Workers Union. Delores Huerta was an elementary school teacher who recognized that her students' struggles in the classroom were not due to lack of effort or ability, but due to lack of resources. Huerta demonstrates that advocating for students and understanding their contexts can help them be better educated. *Picture book.*

References

Adams, J. M. (2016, April 3). *To reach parents, schools try universal language of data*. EdSource. https://edsource.org/2016/to-reach-parents-schools-try-universal-language-of-data/562348

Brady, L., Fryberg, S., Markus, H. R., Griffiths, C., Yang, J., Rodriguez, P., & Mannen-Martinez, L. (2020, December 31). *7 ways for teachers to truly connect with parents*. Education Week. https://www.edweek.org/leader ship/opinion-7-ways-for-teachers-to-truly-connect-with-parents/2020/ 12?utm_source=nl&utm_medium=eml&utm_campaign=eu&M= 59821504&U=&UUID=560b73bce0394a595743cec043ff48ef

Breiseth, L. (2020). *How schools can communicate with ELL families during COVID-19*. ¡Colorín Colorado! https://www.colorincolorado.org/article/ coronavirus-ells-families

¡Colorín Colorado! (n.d.). *Reading tip sheets for parents. https://www.colorincolo-rado.org/reading-tip-sheets-parents*

Elliott, C., Adams, R. J., & Sockalingam, S. (2016a, January 1). *Normative com-munication styles and values for cross-cultural collaboration*. https://www. awesomelibrary.org/multiculturaltoolkit-styleschart-normative.html#

Elliott, C., Adams, R. J., & Sockalingam, S. (2016b, January 1). *Ten myths that prevent collaboration across cultures*. https://www.awesomelibrary.org/ multiculturaltoolkit-myths.html

Family Educational Rights and Privacy Act. (n.d., FERPA). Protecting student privacy. https://studentprivacy.ed.gov/?src=fpco

Gardner, L. (2020a, June 12). *Engaging immigrant & English learner families in a virtual world: 10 lessons learned*. Immigrant Connections. https://www. immigrantsrefugeesandschools.org/post/engaging-immigrant-english-learner-families-in-a-virtual-world-10-lessons-learned

Gardner, L. (2020b, August 2). *How to fulfill interpretation & translation require-ments: Tools for guiding decisions*. Immigrant Connections. https://www. immigrantsrefugeesandschools.org/post/how-to-fulfill-interpretation-translation-requirements-tools-for-guiding-decisions

Lynch, E. W. & Hanson, M. J. (2004). *Developing cross-cultural competence: A guide for working with children and their families* (3rd ed.). Paul H. Brookes.

Mathewson, T. G. (2016, July 2). *Schools are under federal pressure to trans-late for immigrant parents*. Hechinger Report. https://hechingerreport. org/schools-federal-pressure-translate-immigrant-families/

Mexican American Legal Defense and Educational Fund & National Education Association. (2010, June). *Minority parent and community engagement: Best practices and policy recommendations for closing the gaps in student achievement*. http://www.parentcenterhub.org/wp-content/uploads/2016/09/Minority-Parent-and-Community-Engagement_maldef-report_final.pdf

Pew Research Center. (2019, June 12). *Mobile fact sheet*. https://www.pewresearch.org/internet/fact-sheet/mobile/

Reider, K. (2020). *Spark series: Ask Kelly anything!* [Webinar] English Learner Portal. https://www.englishlearnerportal.com/

Sheldon, S. B. & Jung, S. B. (2015, September). *The family engagement partnership student outcome evaluation*. Johns Hopkins University. http://www.pthvp.org/wp-content/uploads/2016/09/JHU-STUDY_FINAL-REPORT.pdf

U.S. Department of Justice & U.S. Department of Education. (2015). *Information for limited English proficient (LEP) parents and guardians and for schools and school districts that communicate with them*. https://www2.ed.gov/about/offices/list/ocr/docs/dcl-factsheet-lep-parents-201501.pdf

Vogels, E. A., Perrin, A., Rainie, L., & Anderson, M. (2020, April 30). *53% of Americans say the internet has been essential during the COVID-19 outbreak*. Pew Research Center. https://www.pewresearch.org/internet/2020/04/30/53-of-americans-say-the-internet-has-been-essential-during-the-covid-19-outbreak/

Weinzapfel, P. [Steven Constantino]. (2020, May 5). *The power of words*. [Video] YouTube. https://www.youtube.com/watch?v=xpvHmVFQios

5

Learning at Home

Scenario: Immigrants Teaching at Home

Nzembo felt lucky that she was able to get a job as a contact tracer during the pandemic in Grand Rapids, Michigan. She wasn't quite fluent in English, but she could speak French and Lingala fluently and some Swahili. Most of all, she could relate with the 8,000 plus Congolese refugees who were now living in Grand Rapids. Most people were distressed to hear from her that they had tested positive for COVID-19 or that they had been exposed and needed to quarantine, but at least, she could explain it in a language they could understand. Her husband, Mobutu, took care of the young children during the day while she locked herself in the bedroom and made calls. The problem was her husband couldn't really help their six-year-old son, Bondeko, with his schoolwork while the school was closed down. She had been able to take free English classes at the refugee center, but he always worked too many hours at a restaurant, which was now closed. He also got frustrated trying to use the tablet that had been provided by the school. As a contact tracer, Nzembo had received computer and internet training and felt comfortable with both. Luckily, Bondeko's teacher recorded her lessons. As soon as she finished working, she and Bondeko would listen to the lesson together, which helped her learn more English too. Then, she would make dinner, and they would work some more. Once a week, someone left a packet on the doorknob with some more lessons for Bondeko, and Mobutu was always good about supervising his son as he completed the lessons during the day and about helping him and his three-year-old sister learn more French, which was his first language. The teacher called the family at least once a week in the evening to check on them and see if they needed any help. It wasn't perfect but they were doing much better than many of the families Nzembo had to call.

Emphasize the Positive

Despite the many challenges of COVID-19, immigrant families and teachers made herculean efforts to continue learning at home. Immigrant families are committed to their children's education. With school support, they can be important partners whether education is going on mostly at home or mostly at school.

> *They too will be teaching their children in important ways that we must not overlook through activities at home, use of the home language, and a focus on critical life lessons… Their talents, networks, and ideas are a rich resource if schools are wise enough to tap into them!*
> (Robertson, 2020, p. 10)

All Families Can Help Their Children Learn

Many immigrant families don't think they can help with their child's education because they do not speak English, or they lack literacy in their home language. Burmese refugees reported wanting to help their children with their schoolwork but not receiving any guidance from the school (Cun, 2020). Therefore, it is important to assure families that regardless of their backgrounds, they can help their children academically.

One way that immigrant families can help their children academically is by speaking and listening to them more in their native language. Genesee (n.d.) lists four advantages to developing the home language as well as English. Research supports higher academic achievement among students who have a strong foundation in their home language, more rapid learning of English, better cognitive skills such as problem solving, and an ability to transfer knowledge and skills from their home language to English. In addition, being bilingual or multilingual is a major advantage in the global economy.

Educators can encourage families to explain to their children what they are doing and why during daily activities, such as housecleaning, cooking, gardening, or car repairs. Younger children can identify colors as family members are doing laundry. If a family member is fixing a leak in a pipe, the child can help hand the parent the needed tools and materials. Although the parent would be speaking in the native language, this example is given in English. The parent might ask for a pipe wrench and explain how it is used to tighten the fittings that hold the pipes together, while pointing to the fittings. Family members should understand that explanations such as these, using as specific words as possible, improve the child's listening skills and expand background knowledge and vocabulary that later can be applied to English reading and writing.

Although immigrants face many challenges, study after study has shown they want their children to receive a good education (Cun, 2020) and they want to help them any way they can.

Asking Families

Whatever the circumstances, it is always important to ask families how the school or teacher can support learning at home rather than assuming the type of support they need (Education Week, 2020). Questions should be framed around student success, but families still may be reluctant to be totally forthright with someone they do not know. For example, the school may ask if they have the internet, and they may answer yes. In reality, they may only have internet on one cell phone, which is with a wage earner outside the house during the day. This emphasizes the importance of developing relationships and asking for ongoing feedback, not just a survey at the beginning of the school year. For example, one unexpected request that came out of the pandemic was for guidance scheduling the student's day, especially when there was more than one student at home trying to study, sharing a device, or sharing limited internet bandwidth (Robertson, 2020).

Home Learning without the Internet

During the pandemic, much of the learning was online, which exposed some of the differences in resources among families. Skelton and Allen (2020) found that many of their emergent bilingual students lacked devices, stable internet, and even regular electricity, especially in rural areas where parents worked in agriculture. Therefore, online learning was not an option for these students at home. Skelton and Allen developed a list of ideas and resources for teaching emergent bilinguals offline that took advantage of their home culture, language, and knowledge. These same resources could be used for homework or summer learning ideas even when school buildings are open.

Families can help develop home language and listening skills by sharing oral stories, songs, or poems. Younger students can make up stories to go with pictures. Older students can read in English and the school can pro-vide families with generic questions in the home language to ask after the reading, such as who was the main character? Would you like to be that character? Why or why not? For non-fiction, what did you learn from this? What questions do you still have about that topic? (Delgado-Gaitan, 2004). If lending books are not available, Skelton and Allen (2020) recommend that educators print things off the internet. For example, NewsELA has printable articles at five different reading levels and activities to go along with the articles.

Students can be asked to keep journals that are provided at the beginning of the school year with different assignments daily. This could go along with assignments from ESL at Home, which provides free non-tech daily lessons for different grade levels in over 30 different languages. Young children might be asked to count shoes and boots or build a ramp and roll things down it one day. Older children might be asked to make up their own superhero with a costume and write about it or find four transparent and four opaque objects in their house.

Scenario: School Bus Hotspot

Ms. Navarro sits in her car close to the school bus every day. There are no face-to-face classes. This is how she gets her children to school. Her three children can get online for their classes through the school bus hotspot. Ms. Navarro has no internet at home, so in order to get her children to school, she has to take time out of her day to make this happen. The kids sit in the car to access their assignments on tablets and laptops provided by the school. Ms. Navarro waits, sometimes making suggestions for her kids as she waits. This is school for her and her family, at least for now.

Online Learning

Digital Challenges

Internet and devices are not distributed equitably. Wan (2020) said that about one in five students said they had trouble accessing assignments remotely during the pandemic. About 60 percent of students who attended low-income Title I schools depended on cell phones to access the internet. Recently, school districts in many areas are partnering with internet providers to expand cov-erage (McNeel, 2020). Although the pandemic brought these issues to light, some online learning in one form or another is probably here to stay.

Issues go beyond device and internet accessibility. Wan (2020) found that about a third of students couldn't get help when they had technology difficulties, and teachers, who were not technology experts, reported spending significant time helping with technology issues. Parents of younger and special needs children also may need extra assistance to use the online learning platforms, such as Seesaw or Livingtree, that are used by schools for instruction and communication. Technology help should be easily available through help desks, hot lines, or simple *how-to* videos with screenshots that show what the computer should look like at each step (Education Week, 2020).

The most common challenge during the pandemic was a lack of a quiet space to work. One reading paraprofessional who was doing a remote one-on-one lesson with a child was amazed at how her student could concentrate with a baby crying and a smoke detector low battery alarm going off in the background. Although this was a particularly difficult time, these same conditions could exist when this child tries to do homework after school.

When discussing online learning and immigrant families, there are some special considerations. Even immigrants who are legally in the country are afraid to apply for free internet or devices because it might affect their immigration cases by indicating they needed public assistance. According to Breiseth (2020), this is not true, but it still has discouraged many families from taking advantage of programs offered throughout the country. One recommendation has been for districts to buy internet plans in bulk for families who lack them or cannot afford the necessary bandwidth or data for online learning (Blackburn, 2020). Another important issue for all families, especially immigrants, is privacy online. If this is the family's first experience with the internet, schools should provide guidelines in their home language about not providing personal information online. The school may also want to avoid asking students to post videos or photos of themselves or family members. Some schools have set up private Facebook pages for specific language groups, which allow them to communicate in relative privacy and in their own languages.

Resources in Languages Other Than English

Gardner (2020b) put together a list of links to tutorial videos in a wide variety of languages for some of the more common platforms to help families learn new technology in their preferred language. For example, there are videos in over 25 languages explaining how to use Google Classroom. Some districts offer online or in-person family academies. Harlingen Independent School District, which is along the Texas–Mexico border, provided parent academies in English and Spanish to help families better understand online instruction during the pandemic. Six-hundred families signed up the first day it was available, which indicates that families will use appropriate assistance when it is offered.

The internet offers many opportunities, especially for emergent bilingual families who may find materials in their preferred language. Online videos, demonstrations, and pictures can help them expand their English vocabulary by associating a visual with new English words or concepts. Gardner (2020a) has compiled a list of videos and websites that provide lessons in a variety of languages. For example, Great Schools has a YouTube Channel organized by subject, grade level, and language (English and Spanish), and Khan Academy has a playlist in English, Spanish, French, and Brazilian Portuguese. Unite for Literacy has books that are narrated in 45 different languages, and International Children's Digital Library has children's books from all over the world representing their culture and language. (See online support materials.)

Hybrid Learning

During the pandemic, many schools went to some form of hybrid or blended learning. Even online learning might be partially synchronous, with the teacher live, and partially asynchronous, with the students working independently on material posted online. This has sparked renewed discussions about what type of instruction or practice requires interaction with the teacher and what can be done independently (Arnett, 2020). This is particularly important for immigrant families and students because adults may not be able to help students with assignments in English. According to Arnett, students can learn facts and basic concepts independently with appropriate online programs, videos, and practice. Teachers are important for helping students with any misunderstandings and higher order thinking, such as analysis and problem solving. Teachers may also want to focus their time and efforts on students struggling academically or emotionally while allowing other students to work at their own pace independently and encouraging them to pursue personal interests with regular feedback.

Scenario: Challenges Faced at Home

Mrs. Tucker had twins, Larissa and Marissa, in her fourth-grade class. Every day, the twins arrived at school on the bus, neatly dressed and groomed. Although they spoke Spanish as their first language in kindergarten, they had learned to speak, read, and write well in English by fourth grade. In fact, they came in after lunch one day a week to help with the school newspaper. They did well academically and always had their homework done before school—that is until early November. Suddenly, both girls stopped doing their homework even though they were still coming to school daily and doing well during school. Mrs. Tucker asked them if anything was wrong, but the girls just said they didn't have time to do their homework. Concerned after a couple of weeks of missing homework, Mrs. Tucker decided to make a home visit. As she pulled up to the mobile home far north of town and a long bus drive from school, she immediately knew what the problem was. They didn't have electricity. They had propane for heat, cooking, and hot water, but they lacked electricity for lights. The girls had done their homework regularly until early November because that was when daylight savings ended, and it was now dark by the time they arrived home.

Although this real scenario is extreme, it does point out that teachers often do not understand the adversities that children and their families face at home. It also shows the tremendous effort that some families must make to keep their children healthy, clean, fed, clothed, and at school each day. Not all families have the same resources available for homework or participating in the education of their children, yet they still want the best education possible for their children. Many families also live in small crowded apartments or mobile homes, where it is difficult for students to concentrate or find a quiet place to work. All these factors should be considered as assignments are given and grading is completed for work done at home.

Traditional Homework

Proponents of homework, given when school is face-to-face, argue that it provides extra practice on strategies taught at school, that it improves the connection between school and home, and that it teaches students responsibility. However, studies are questioning all of those assumptions.

There is no evidence that homework in elementary school or middle school improves achievement, and there is just a small improvement in achievement in high school (Kohn, 2006). Although it is generally assumed that homework teaches responsibility, there is no research that supports that conclusion. As mentioned above, there are often factors beyond students' control that impact their ability to do homework.

Not only are the benefits of homework much less than generally assumed, but there are negative effects of homework, especially too much homework. Homework takes time away from other activities and erodes family relations. Family members want to make sure they meet the expectations of the school by having their children do homework, but it often ends up in battles over completing homework before doing other activities, even eating dinner

(Dudley-Marling, 2003). Instead of improving school–home connections, homework often creates resentment toward teachers and schools.

Rather than requiring a specific amount of homework each day, teachers should assign homework when it will extend classroom learning without causing undue stress on students or families. Some school districts also have reduced the consequences of not completing homework. When a large percentage of a grade is based on homework, students may understand concepts but receive low grades simply because they do not finish their homework due to circumstances beyond their control.

Based on the information available about homework, educators should ask themselves some questions about homework policies:

- What is the purpose of homework?
- Does the amount and type of homework being given support that purpose?
- How is homework affecting students' grades and opportunities at school?
- Is homework adapted for English learners (ELs) or struggling students?
- Is homework appropriate for students who lack resources at home?
- Is homework likely to create resentment or closer relations within families?

The activities suggested below are ways of including homework that works from the strengths of the families as well as developing skills.

Connect Families with Community Help

Most immigrant families recognize their limitations in assisting their children with schoolwork and will take advantage of help when it is available (Cun, 2020; Delgado-Gaitan, 2004). The authors and their college students had an after-school tutoring program at a local public school. Once the families found out about the program, there was a waiting list to get in. Immigrant families made sure that their children came every week because the limited spots would be taken by someone else if they missed more than once. Although the program was designed to assist students with reading and writing, families often asked tutors to help their child with math or other homework; explain a letter or report that had come home from school; or discuss what a person needed to do to get into college. Thus, if schools provide assistance for immigrant families, they will take advantage of the help. This assistance may come in the form of other parents, community volunteers, high school or college students who volunteer to help, or organizations such as the Boys and Girls Club or refugee assistance centers. Information about the assistance program should be provided in the native languages of the community and efforts should be made to find bilingual parents who will pass the word on to other families who speak the same native language.

Activity: Family Interviews

Purpose: People have busy lives, and few take time to really talk with their children. This activity encourages children to speak with older members of the family, including parents, grandparents, or other people who are important to them.

Participants: Student and an older family member. This activity is appropriate for third grade through high school.

Preparation and resources: Either the school or students should prepare questions in the home language in advance. Students will need paper and pencil.

Description of activity: The student asks questions of an older family member. These questions may be about what school was like when they were a child, what type of work they have done, what they did with their friends when they were young, what things have been invented since they were a child, where they grew up, or anything else of interest. The student should only ask a few questions at a time, so this may be an activity that is repeated with different questions throughout the year. The student takes notes of the family member's responses in either the home language or English. The student next writes up what he or she learned in his or her home language or English and shares it with the teacher. If the interview is not written in English, the student translates the interview into English and shares it with the class. If there is someone else in the class who shares the same native language, those students may want to work together on translating their interviews.

Options: Students can take turns taking a recorder home so they can record their interviews.

Or the child could take a photo with a cell phone and email it to the teacher to print out. These photographs can then be printed and placed with the interview. Students can do additional research on one aspect of the interview. For example, the student can learn about one of the inventions that occurred in that person's lifetime or about the community where that person was born. Be sensitive to privacy issues.

Activity: Grocery Store Math

Purpose: The grocery store offers many opportunities to develop math concepts ranging from basic counting to more complex percentages. This should be done during the family's regular trip to the grocery store.

Participants: Family members and students. Activities can be adapted for prekindergarten through high school.

Preparation and resources: Notes should be sent home in the native language explaining the assignment. The teacher may also want to provide a special sheet for recording findings. Students will need paper and pencil and perhaps a calculator.

Description of activity: The student goes to the grocery store with the family member. Based on the instructions sent home, the family member asks the student to do math related to the shopping (see options below). The student reports back to the teacher what they did at the grocery store.

Options: There are many options for activities, such as:

◆ Young students can be asked to count items. For example, the family member may say they need five apples, and the child finds and counts five apples.

◆ Have students weigh fruits and vegetables sold by the pound and determine what the cost will be for the amount being purchased.

◆ Older students can be taught to look at prices per ounce on signs and compare them for similar products.

◆ Students can determine how much is needed of items. For example, if two hot dog buns are needed for each member of a six-person family and the buns come in packages of eight, how many packages do you need to buy?

◆ Determine the price of items after taking the advertised discount. For example, if an item is 20 percent off, what will be the price of the item after taking off the 20 percent?

◆ Determine the price of items after taking a coupon discount. How does this price compare to other brands without the coupon?

◆ Use a calculator and keep track of the total cost of items placed in the cart. How does this compare to the actual cost at checkout?

Activity: Nutrition and Health

Purpose: Nutrition and health are important to students and their families. This activity helps students become more aware of nutritional facts of the foods they commonly eat at home and involves families in the student's investigation. (Immigrants often have trouble finding ingredients they are used to cooking in local stores.)

Participants: Students and a family member. This activity can be modified for prekindergarten through high school.

Preparation and resources: If possible, notes should go home explaining the homework in the home language. The teacher may want to begin the unit on food and nutrition before students get items from home. The teacher needs a large chart with the food groups labeled and with space for students to write in at the students' level. Internet access, books, or other materials about nutrition should be available.

Description of activity: A student and a family member find one nonperishable food item in a box, bag, or can for the student to bring to school. The student shares the item from home with the class. The class then determines where the item fits on the food chart and the student writes or draws it in the correct spot on the chart. The child takes the food item home and tells the family where he/she put it on the chart. Upper elementary, middle school, and high school students can share information from the nutritional label. Items also can be categorized by their fat, sodium, carbohydrate, fiber, sugar, or protein content. After information is collected on a number of food items, the class can discuss how they could create a balanced meal.

Options: After students have studied the nutritional content of food, ask them to find something that is high in a specific characteristic, such as sodium, sugar, or protein. Students can compare the nutritional characteristics of similar items, such as tuna packed in water with tuna packed in oil; crackers with cookies; or pinto beans with black beans. Students can also be encouraged to go to the grocery store with family members and help them find low-cost, nutritional foods. Teachers can give students a worksheet on which they copy down nutritional information at home rather than bringing the item to school. A similar nutrition activity could be done online.

Activity: Online Read-Alouds

Purpose: This can help emergent bilingual family members as well as students learn English vocabulary and reading.

Participants: Family members and student.

Preparation and resources: Students and family members should be introduced to the website and how to use it. It should not be a required activity at home if not all families have access to devices with internet.

Description of activity: Go to Storyline Online (www.storylineonline.net). This website has stories for children read by members of the Screen Actors Guild. The text and pictures are visible as the actors read the stories aloud. Choose a story and listen to it. Complete related activities if desired.

Options: Have families complete a log of stories and activities. Provide other free internet sites where families can see the text as it is read aloud.

Activity: Technology for Families

Purpose: By providing sessions about technology, schools can help increase family's technology skills and discover what obstacles families face in using technology at home for communication and homework. Care must be taken not to embarrass any families who do not have smartphones or high-speed internet.

Participants: Families with children, teachers, at least one technology specialist, and some high school students as volunteers.

Preparation and resources: Find out what families are particularly interested in learning in advance. Using the school platform or website? Do they want to know about using phones to locate their children? Blocking certain sites? Keeping their children safe from cyberbullying? Managing Facebook, Twitter, Instagram, email, and other accounts? Safe websites for research or educational sites for young children?

Choose one or two topics. Invite families in their home language and let them know what to bring. If families are going to use their own cell phones, laptops, or tablets, make sure they can access the internet at the school. If they are going to use school computers, the school should have computers or a computer lab internet ready for the families. There is nothing more frustrating than not having the technology work. Have a technology specialist on hand to trouble-shoot and have smaller sessions if necessary, for easier Wi-Fi access. Prepare tip sheets and/or lists of appropriate websites for families to take home in their home language.

Description of activity: Begin with an age appropriate 15–20-minute presentation. Either have presentations for different language groups in different rooms or group families by language in the main room and have an interpreter near each group or use headsets. Do an interactive activity with devices. Use high school students to help families get on the internet and complete activities.

Options: Make a list of appropriate websites that are available in languages other than English and help families explore them.

Activity: Vocabulary Expansion from Home

Purpose: This activity encourages students to learn the names of everyday items they have in their homes and find out how they are used. Thus, it promotes conversation among family members in their home language. This activity is based on suggestions made in *Classrooms that Work* by Cunningham and Allington (2011).

Participants: Students and family members, prekindergarten through high school.

Preparation and resources: If possible, notes should be sent in the home language explaining the homework assignment. Teachers will need a camera, computer, printer with colored ink, index cards, and space on the wall or bulletin board to display the photos and captions.

Description of activity: The teacher will ask the student to find a particular type of item at home. The student and a family member will then try to find one of these items at home and discuss how it is used. Examples for categories include: kitchen implements, tools, balls, soaps, things made of metal or wood, homemade items, and many more. The student will then share the item with the class and discuss how it is used in his or her home. For example, one child may say her mom uses a rolling pin for tortillas, while another may say his dad uses it for pies. Thus, everyone's vocabulary and background knowledge expand. Students make personal connections to the vocabulary. A digital photograph is taken of the item and printed out. The child writes the name of the item and how it is used on an index card, which is placed under the photo on the bulletin board. Assign different children different days to bring in their items so that 20 or more children are not trying to share their item in one day.

Options: A few students a day can share items from a particular category online. Make sure students and families, if appropriate, know what the category is, so it doesn't become a competition of the newest or best toys or electronics.

The teacher can identify an item in the classroom, such as *hinges* on the door, which may be a term the child does not know. The child can then share the English term with his family and ask what the term is in their home language if it is not known. They can then count how many they have in the house or apartment together. Young students may be asked to bring an item, picture, or drawing of something that begins with a specific sound, thus reinforcing the phonics lesson from class.

If you have a family member who would like to volunteer at school but doesn't speak English, he or she can help take photographs, print them out, and place them on the bulletin board. The family member can even put the name for the item in his or her home language on the index card along with the English name

Relevant Literature

The Journey, by Francesca Sanna (2016), describes a refugee child's story about traveling from a war-torn country, where the father has died, to a new home. It requires the mother and children to leave everything behind and travel by cars, trucks, bicycles, foot, boat, and train. The story's narrator notes, "the farther we go… the more we leave behind." The setting is not specific in terms of a region or country and ends with hope for the family in their new home and land. *Picture book.*

The Namesake, by Lahiri Jhumpa (2004), is about a family in which the parents are from the West Bengal region of India, and the children are born in the United States. The story describes the clash between generations and cultures over more than 30 years. The narrative includes some of the misunderstandings that occur with the schools, especially the use of Gogol's home name at school instead of his "good" name. The schools are unaware of the education the children are receiving at home, including weekly lessons in reading and writing the parents' native Bengali language. While the children are assimilated to American culture, the parents, especially the mother, are much more tied to their native India, and most of their friends came from the same area that they did. *Chapter book.*

References

Arnett, T. (2020, July 20). *Revisiting blended learning principles with school plans in limbo*. EdSurge. https://www.edsurge.com/news/2020-07-20-revisiting-blended-learning-principles-with-school-plans-in-limbo

Blackburn, S. (2020, August 5). *4 best practices for more equitable internet access*. District Administration. https://districtadministration.com/4-best-practices-for-more-equitable-internet-access/

Breiseth, L. (2020). *How to expand ELLs' access to technology for distance learning*. ¡Colorín Colorado! https://www.colorincolorado.org/article/distance-learning-ell-technology

Cun, A. (2020). Concerns and expectations: Burmese refugee parents' perspectives on their children's learning in American schools. *Early Childhood Education Journal* 48, 263–272. https://doi.org/10.1007/s10643-019-00983-z

Cunningham, P. M. & Allington, R. L. (2011). *Classrooms that work: They can all read and write* (4th ed.). Pearson.

Delgado-Gaitan, C. (2004). *Involving Latino families in school.* Corwin.

Dudley-Marling, C. (2003, March). How school troubles come home: The impact of homework on families of struggling learners. *Current Issues in Education*, 6, 1–19. https://www.researchgate.net/publication/286944183_How_school_troubles_come_home_The_impact_of_homework_on_families_of_struggling_learners

Education Week. (2020, August 12). *How educators can help parents: 6 remote learning tips.* https://www.edweek.org/ew/section/multimedia/how-educators-can-help-parents-6-remote.html

Gardner, L. (2020a, March 26). *English learner family engagement during Coronavirus.* Immigrant Connections. https://www.immigrantsrefugees andschools.org/post/english-learner-family-engagement-during-coronavirus

Gardner, L. (2020b, May 14). *Google Classroom and more in multiple languages.* Immigrant Connections. https://www.immigrantsrefugeesandschools. org/post/google-classroom-and-more-in-multiple-languages

Genesee, F. (n.d.). *The home language: An English language learner's most valuable resource.* ¡Colorín Colorado! https://www.colorincolorado.org/article/ home-language-english-language-learners-most-valuable-resource #comment-3000

Kohn, A. (2006). *Does homework improve learning?* https://www.alfiekohn. org/homework-improve-learning/

McNeel, B. (2020, July 14). *Closing San Antonio's digital divide: In the city's poorest and most segregated neighborhoods. Public school students get in-home internet.* The 74. https://www.the74million.org/article/closing-san-antonios-digital-divide-in-the-citys-poorest-and-most-segregated-neighborhoods-public-school-students-to-get-in-home-internet/

Robertson, K. (2020). *Distance learning for ELLs: Lessons learned about family partnerships.* ¡Colorín Colorado! https://www.colorincolorado.org/ article/distance-learning-ells-family

Skelton, B. & Allen, M. A. (2020). *Offline learning at home: Ideas for English language learners.* ¡Colorín colorado! https://www.colorincolorado.org/article/ offline-learning-ells

Wan, T. (2020, July 22). *Report: One of the biggest obstacles to remote learning? Finding a quiet place to work.* EdSurge. https://www.edsurge.com/news/ 2020-07-22-report-one-of-the-biggest-obstacles-to-remote-learning-finding-a-quiet-place-to-work

6

Beyond Open Houses

Scenario: Positive Meeting

Ricardo's teacher was having a family meeting tonight from 7 to 8 p.m. Ricardo's mom, Patricia, always looked forward to these meetings, which gave her time to have dinner with her children and still get them to bed at a reasonable hour after the meeting. Best of all, the teacher encouraged her to bring Ricardo and his younger sister, Marisa, with her. When they arrived in the first-grade classroom, the desks had been moved to the side and adult-sized folding chairs had been placed in a semicircle. In front of the chairs was a large rug area. Ms. Sandoval greeted everyone and then encouraged the children to sit on the rug and the adults to sit on the chairs, grouped by language. She used a big book in English to demonstrate how to do a read-aloud, beginning by looking at the cover and title and making predictions about what the story would be about. Then, she read and showed the pictures to the children on the rug, making sure to stop and point out important points but not stop so often they would lose the story line.

After she finished reading, she asked the children if the book reminded them of anything in their lives. A parent who spoke English and Spanish and a parent who spoke English and Somali volunteered to paraphrase important points to the parents who did not speak English and translate their comments or questions. Ms. Sandoval also explained how to make up stories to go with a picture book if the child brought home a book in English that no one at home could read.

Then, everyone helped Ms. Sandoval move the chairs into a circle with the chairs facing outward and put a number on each chair. In the meantime, she placed a variety of picture books in English, Spanish, and Somali out on a table at the side of the room. Family members and students walked around the outside of the circle of chairs to the music. When the music stopped, Ricardo would find a seat and Ms. Sandoval would pull two numbers out of a jar. The students on the chairs with those numbers got to choose a book from the table to take home. Chairs and numbers were removed until there were only four students and their families walking around the circle. Ms. Sandoval made sure there were enough books for all the students in her class as well as their siblings who had come to the meeting. Ms. Sandoval pointed out the sign-up sheet for conferences on her desk and encouraged families who wanted to learn about the progress of their child to sign up for an individual confidential conference. Patricia signed up for a Sunday afternoon conference with the teacher. As families left, Ms. Sandoval handed out tips about reading aloud to your child in English, Spanish, and Somali.

Ms. Sandoval's meeting engaged immigrant families in many ways. Instead of just telling families how to do a read-aloud, she demonstrated it and included the children in the discussion. The session was targeted for families of first graders, but she made sure to include siblings in the activities. Each family went home with books and a tip sheet in their native language. She also kept the meeting short so that it would not disrupt the family schedule too much.

Although traditional open houses or back-to-school nights are well-meaning, they often fall short in a number of ways. They tend to focus on the school providing information rather than partnering with families. The same information is often provided throughout the year and to families with children at all different grade levels. Families may go home empty handed rather than with ideas they can implement. There are many ways of making family meetings more engaging for everyone, especially immigrant families (Table 6.1).

What Families Want

Different families need and want different things from the school (see Chapter 2). When schools are not responsive to family's interests, they are sending the message that schools know better than the families themselves what they need (Knackendoffel et al., 2017). This can lead to a negative cycle in which families don't think their ideas or opinions are valued and come to fewer events at school (Mexican American Legal Defense and Educational

Table 6.1 Guidelines for Successful Events

- Ask families what they would like to do at these events.
- Offer family sessions at different times and different days.
- Offer sessions in different locations and online.
- Invite families with notes in their preferred language.
- Make sure the meeting is interactive. Families should not just be passive listeners.
- Plan for simultaneous interpretation through headphones or sessions in different languages in different rooms or on different days. Avoid doing sessions in English and then interpreting word for word in another language.
- Provide information or materials that families can use at home.
- Have sign-up sheets for families who want to speak with the teacher individually about their child.
- Provide contact information for the school and teacher.
- Respect families who do not come to school.

Fund & National Education Association, 2010). School officials then believe the families are not interested in their children's education and don't make an effort to involve them. The only way to break this cycle is to respond to families' different requests and be sensitive to their needs.

Language

One of the biggest obstacles to immigrant families participating in school events is language. Language barriers for events can be bridged in a number of ways but first schools need to know what languages parents want to use with the school. More information about interpretation and translation is included in Chapter 4.

Different Types of Events

Schools, families, and community members can partner for a great variety of events depending on the preferences of the families. These can vary from events that are mostly created for goodwill such as drive-in movie nights or cookouts to serious sessions such as talking to your children about racism. Five different types of events are described here: helping immigrant families understand U.S. schools, breaking down stereotypes, online workshops, community partnerships, and family leadership preparation. One activity representing each of these topics is included at the end of the chapter.

Helping Immigrant Families Understand U.S. Schools

Educators may ask if immigrants should be included with other families in larger events or have small events targeted to their specific needs. Gardner (2019b) says schools should do both. Large events involving both immigrants and native-born Americans should be carefully crafted to allow the groups to get to know each other (see *Breaking Down Stereotypes* below).

Smaller events can be targeted toward needs identified by immigrant families and be presented in their preferred languages.

School systems are different in other countries, and U.S. expectations and procedures are strange to many newcomers. For example, some recent immigrant families in the Washington, D.C. area requested orientation for families as well as students (Colón, 2017). Immigrant families could be grouped by language with an interpreter, who has been given information for each location in advance. The groups would visit classrooms, the office, cafeteria, gym, library, nurse's office, pick-up areas, and other important locations. At each location, the school should provide information in the home language about school procedures, such as how to pay for school lunches or more complex issues like giving or denying permission for someone else to pick up the child. Families should also have time to ask questions. As with all school events, sign-up sheets for individual conferences and contact information should be provided.

Explanations and modeling of various language programs such as English as a second language, transitional bilingual instruction, dual language, and all English classes are important to many immigrant families (Table 6.2). Other possible topics for immigrant family events are parent–teacher conference procedures, use of the school website or platform, special academic programs, and transitions to middle school and high school. Standardized assessments are also unfamiliar to many immigrant families yet can impact their child's life in numerous ways. An activity about assessments can be found at the end of the chapter.

Breaking Down Stereotypes

Many family engagement programs are based on White middle-class family values and often marginalize minority and immigrant families (Williamson & Blackburn, 2016). Educators, staff, and families have stereotypes about each other. Parents "are aware of the stereotypes present among school employees and other parents and may resist participating in parent activities where those stereotypes may be displayed" (paragraph 11).

When families from different ethnic backgrounds do not have personal interaction, it is easy to stereotype other groups. Author Muhammad (2019) calls it being "othered." Although it may not seem like the schools' responsibility

Table 6.2 Different Types of School Language Programs

Transitional Bilingual Programs	Dual Language Programs	English as a Second Language
Students receive instruction in their native language and English with increasing amounts of English instruction.	Dual language programs include native English speakers with native speakers of another language, and both learn the other language while maintaining their native language.	All instruction is conducted in English with extra supports, such as objects and photos to increase vocabulary. This is often used when there are not enough students of the same language background for a bilingual class.

to break down these stereotypes in the community, the attitudes of parents can spill over into the schools and "negatively affect overall campus atmosphere and academic performance" (Mexican American Legal Defense and Educational Fund & National Education Association, 2010, p. 36).

One of the strategies the report recommends is designing a program where families from different cultural backgrounds exchange ideas about common issues such as controlling screen time and content, bullying, or finding inexpensive things to do in the community. In Los Angeles, they used *house meetings* to discuss common concerns (Auerbach, 2009). These are smaller meetings in classrooms where ideas are shared. Through family story sharing, teachers learn more about the families they serve, families are empowered, and they learn from each other. The house meetings in Los Angeles have been especially successful in building relationships with culturally and linguistically diverse families who might otherwise be hesitant to approach the school and share concerns. Care must be taken that a few people do not dominate the discussion.

Immigrants and native-born Americans also can work together on projects so they can get to know each other better. The projects could be gardening, creating after-school activities, or designing safety programs. "Immigrant parents learn about others living in their new community and ideally, those who have lived in the community for years learn a bit about the cultural backgrounds of their new neighbors" (Gardner, 2019b, p. 2). The *Missing Pieces of the Curriculum Activity* at the end of the chapter is an example of this type of activity.

Online Workshops

During the pandemic, most schools in the United States moved online for both student instruction and family engagement. Advantages and disadvantages emerged that will guide the use of online engagement activities for many years.

Families appreciated online workshops because they didn't require them to go anywhere or find childcare. It is also possible for educators to record the sessions and allow later comments so families who are not available for the live workshop could participate at a more convenient time. One of the biggest problems with online workshops is not all families have the necessary computers or broadband to participate fully (Lazarín, 2020). According to Lazarín at the Migration Policy Institute, many immigrants depend on their cell phones and data plans for online activities.

Online workshops also tend to be more lectures than interactive workshops. There are a number of formats that can make online workshops more interactive. One is to set up a watch party of a short interesting video with voice-over in other languages. Families can then respond in the chat box in their own languages and a translator can provide the comments in English.

Another format is to give families a short assignment to do before the online workshop, such as drawing a picture of a place they like to visit or writing a poem about their family. Children and adults can work together on the assignment. Then, during the workshop, each family has a brief opportunity to share what they prepared, which is also a good way to share cultures.

The third possible interactive format is one where the teacher briefly instructs the family on a topic and they do it at home. This could be writing Haiku, using a free grocery store flyer to do math problems, solving logic puzzles, making Origami, or learning a song or rap. The online activity at the end of the chapter is a science experiment that can be done with simple household items.

Community Partnerships

Community–school partnerships offer many advantages, especially when engaging immigrant families (¡Colorín Colorado!, 2018). Community organizations have insights into challenges families are facing and knowledge of services in the community that may help them with housing, food, jobs, health care, legal, and other services. They may have volunteers who can speak the families' home languages. EMBARC (Ethnic Minorities of Burma Advocacy and Resource Center) in Iowa offers information in ten different Asian and African languages spoken in the community. When community groups partner with schools for events, the expenses and planning are shared too.

One way for schools to partner with community organizations is for the school to provide space for community organizations to offer classes to immigrant families and others at the school. The school can offer after-school programs for students while the parents take classes, such as GED, English as a second language, computers, or citizenship. As with all family interactions, community–school partnerships should be based on the expressed interests of the families (see Chapter 2). Many organizations are eager to reach out to more families in the community. The partnerships take many different forms. For example, orchestras, zoos, local theaters, or nature centers may offer free or low-cost admission to families on certain days. Or community organizations may sponsor special programs, such as housing fairs, voter information and registration, college fairs, or concerts. After a health presentation, nursing aids could be available to do basic blood pressure, oxygen, and eyesight checks. They would have information available for those who needed follow-up. These may be one-day events or ongoing partnerships (see more ideas for partnerships in Chapters 9 and 10).

Activities may be conducted at the school or in the community. Places of worship are often the focal point of neighborhoods and can offer facilities for non-religious school activities that will attract families who might not come to the school. Meeting rooms at neighborhood community centers or libraries are other alternatives for neighborhood-based events. The *Job Fair Activity* at the end of the chapter is an example of school and community collaboration.

Family Leadership Preparation

One of the things missing in most school relationships with immigrant families is family leadership preparation (Gardner, 2019a). Having immigrant families in leadership and advocacy positions benefits schools, students, and families (¡Colorín Colorado!, 2018). Leaders from immigrant communities can provide a connection between those communities and the school, the district, and even the school board. They also can bring hidden issues to light. Some examples are explaining barriers to immigrant family participation with the school, suggesting specific safety and anti-bullying measures, advocating for more multilingual counselors and social workers, and promoting ethnically sensitive curriculum and staff.

Many families never feel ready or have the time to take leadership positions, but schools owe it to interested families to provide them with preparation and to really listen to their concerns. Han and Love (2015) call these people "Cultural Leaders" and consider that to be the highest level of family engagement and important to building trust between immigrant communities and schools. Many organizations have leadership training information available online, including the Parent Teacher Association (PTA), which has advocacy training manuals in both English and Spanish.

Odyssey Elementary School in Everett, Washington, used the Washington Alliance for Better Schools' Natural Leaders Program to provide preparation for community leaders. They now have three Spanish speakers and one

Russian/Ukrainian speaker who have lists of families they reach out to in their communities. They provide information, translation services, and even have small neighborhood meetings. Principal Cheryl Boze says, "It used to be that parents who weren't native speakers hardly came to any school events and now they are so much more comfortable" (National Association of Elementary School Principals, 2008, p. 6). Other organizations that promote family leadership preparation are discussed in Chapter 10. This chapter makes suggestions in the leadership and advocacy activities at the end of the chapter.

Activity: Job Fair

Purpose: When schools hold job fairs on campus or co-host them elsewhere, they show students that they understand the importance that students and their families place on finding after-school and weekend work, summer jobs, and full-time employment after graduation.

Participants: High school students legally old enough to work and their families, employment experts, potential employers.

Preparation and resources: Arrange tables near electrical outlets where potential employers and others can set up their displays. Make arrangements for non-English speakers either by having headsets and interpreters for the main presentation or separate presentations in home languages in different rooms.

Description of activity: Have a speaker talk for about 20 minutes about ways of finding appropriate employment, resumes, applications, interviews, and other related topics. While the speaker is talking in one room, employers and other job-related agencies can set up tables in a separate room. Stations can be provided where students can talk with potential employers, military recruiters, and employment services. There can be other stations where students receive help with their resumes and practice interview skills one-on-one. Provide a bulleted list of job-finding tips in the home languages of the families.

Options: Some schools have work–study programs in which high school students spend part of their school day working in the community. Counselors may set up a table to discuss these programs with students and families.

Activities: Leadership and Advocacy Preparation

Purpose: To prepare family members for leadership and advocacy roles. This is especially important for groups of families who are usually not represented in leadership roles in the school or district. After the workshops, these cultural leaders can then be asked to serve in volunteer or even paid positions that take advantage of their skills and knowledge. For example, they could serve on Bilingual Parent Advisory Committees or Special Education Advisory Committees.

Participants: Family members, especially from underrepresented groups. Interpreters as appropriate. A facilitator. This could be a school administrator, a university leadership instructor or graduate student, or someone from a community advocacy group, such as Community Organizing and Family Issues (COFI, https://cofionline.org/COFI/).

Possible Activities: Leadership involves many different skills. Schools may want to have a series of family leadership workshops with hands-on activities at each workshop. Try to make each workshop a stand-alone activity, so families will benefit if they cannot attend all the workshops. Have interpreters available as needed. The following are some ideas.

Letter and Email Writing: Discuss choosing a topic, considering your audience, supporting your opinion with facts, providing your own contact information, and other letter writing tactics. Then, encourage families to write a letter or email to a teacher, principal, school board member, or the local newspaper about a topic important to them. Have translators available as needed.

Working with the media: Have a member of the media come to the school and discuss with the family leaders what they are looking for in events or ideas that they include in their newspaper, radio station, TV station, podcast… This might include a calendar of events, letters to the editor, and on-site coverage of a school activity. How should the family leaders pitch their ideas to the media?

Organizing events: Work together on planning an event for families. A school administrator should be assigned to the group for this activity, so the group can obtain reliable information about facilities, conflicting events, and liability issues. Discuss important aspects of the event, such as inclusion and making it interactive. After the group has decided what type of event to have, choose possible dates and times, which will be considered by the administrator. After discussing the different roles, divide the work among participants: event coordinator, publicity and invitations, getting necessary speakers and/or materials, obtaining the venue and making sure it is ready on the event date, greeting participants, organizing the actual event, clean-up, and evaluating the success of the event. The event coordinator should know how to contact the administrator as questions and problems arise.

Commenting at a meeting: Discuss choosing a topic, focusing and limiting comments, and including facts that might sway the listener. Have family members choose a topic and practice with each other doing three-minute presentations as they might do at a school board meeting.

Speaking with a decision maker: Discuss changes the family leaders would like to see in the school or community and list them so all the family members can see. Choose one for your focus. What points can be made to support this change? List them. What would someone who was opposed to this change say? List them. Then, have family members role play both the decision maker and the family group wanting changes. If possible, invite a decision maker to a future workshop and present the ideas to him or her.

Working with existing family groups: If there are established family groups on campus, such as PTA, Parent Teacher Organization (PTO) or booster clubs, invite leaders from the groups to one of the workshops. Have them discuss the types of activities they do. Have them explain to workshop participants how they could join the existing organizations or collaborate with them.

Activity: Missing Pieces of the Curriculum

Purpose: Families frequently say they wish students learned more about _____ in school. This is a good opportunity to have immigrant families and American-born families work together on a common goal. Trust will be built when everyone works to identify things they believe are missing in the curriculum. It is important that this is an on-going activity and that families believe their concerns are taken seriously.

Participants: Families and educators, including an administrator. Limit the grade levels engaged at one time. High school student volunteers who can greet families in needed languages. Interpreters. Someone who will type into the computer during the workshop.

Preparation and resources: Reserve a large room with tables, such as a cafeteria. Have a microphone available, a computer, a projector, and a screen. Each table should have a large number on it for seating purposes. Each table also should have a list with five spaces for the groups' top issues and a pen or pencil. Later in the workshop, index cards and pens or pencils for each participant will be needed.

Send invitations home and post on the school platform and website in home languages. Have childcare available at the school or crayons and paper available at the tables for parents who bring young children with them. Older children can participate in the activities. Ask families to send an RSVP with the number of people coming, including children, and the language they prefer using. Assign families to tables in advance. For example, table 8 might be designated as an English and Spanish table with an English–Spanish interpreter. If possible, also mix people who grew up in the United States with immigrants from countries such as Uganda and Nigeria where they also speak English. Appropriate personnel may need to reach out to cultural leaders from immigrant communities if they did not respond to invitations.

Description of activity: High school students who speak a language other than English should help greet the families and guide them to their assigned table. A school administrator should introduce the topic and tell families that the school wants to know what they believe students should know but are not currently learning. The school hopes to work with them on their ideas, although it will take time. Encourage families to discuss their ideas, such as Black historical figures, reasons immigrants come to the United States, understanding people with special needs, art, or chess. Have each table come up with their top five suggestions. Have the interpreter or one person from each group share their top idea, which will then be recorded on the computer and projected onto the screen. If the top suggestion is already mentioned, the group should share their second idea and so forth. When all groups have shared, ask if there are other major suggestions that have not been mentioned. Try to combine ideas when appropriate and reduce them to four or five topics but make sure that at least some minority group suggestions remain. Provide index cards to each participant and ask them to put down their name, top two ideas that they would like to work on, preferred language, and contact information. Thank them for their input and announce the next meeting date or tell them how they will be contacted.

Identify educators or other staff members who would be willing to work on each topic. The next workshops should be conducted in separate rooms divided by topic or on separate dates. Begin with the core group that was interested in the topic according to their index card and make sure immigrant families feel included by providing interpreters as needed. As much as possible, the discussion should be led by families to brainstorm specific ideas of what should be included and where information or assistance might be found. For example, if families wanted more discussion of Hispanic figures, perhaps there is a local affiliate of UnidosUS (https://www.unidosus.org/) that might be willing to help. Some ideas such as a chess or art club may require after-school or weekend programs and community help.

Follow-up, even if it is not all positive, is essential or families will believe their ideas are being ignored and won't come to future meetings.

Options: Other topics for shared decision-making might be campus budget, beautification, bullying, after-school activities, or safety issues.

Activity: Standardized Testing

Purpose: Standardized testing has become more common at all grade levels across the country and has greater impact on children and their families than ever before. One state report for parents includes scale scores, confidence intervals, and some item analysis. All of this information is not very helpful if family members do not understand the information.

Families want to know what is assessed, how it is assessed, how they can help their children do better on the assessment, how to interpret the scores, and what impact the scores will have on their children's future. For example, few Spanish-speaking countries use any type of early assessment and rarely use the type of standardized assessments found in the United States.

Participants: Families, educators, and interpreters who can explain assessments clearly in the languages needed.

Preparation and resources: Varies with the activities chosen.

Description of activity: Explain how to read test scores. Most schools give different assessments at different grade levels, so separate sessions should be conducted for families of children taking each of the different assessments. Provide examples of pretend test scores projected on a screen. Explain what each score means and allow families to ask questions. Then, explain the significance of each score. Families want to know what happens when children do exceptionally well or poorly on the assessment. Will children be recommended for more diagnostic testing when they receive certain scores? What assistance does the school provide to students who score poorly on the assessment?

Soon after explaining the scoring system to a large group of families, educators should meet individually with families who want to review their child's last test score. These conferences need to be confidential, conducted away from other families, and conducted in the families' dominant language. Many times, families receive scores but do not know how these scores compare to others at the same grade level or what the scores mean in terms of the child's future. Since standardized tests are often used to make decisions about retention and special needs programs, it is important that families know how to interpret the scores. These conferences could be set up at the same time as other families participate in activities or sign-up sheets could be provided for conferences at a later date.

Families can go from station to station to learn about the different components of the tests and what they can do at home to assist their children. Even if the child is being tested in English, families should be provided with ideas of things they can do at home in their native language. For example, the child might read something in English, but a family member could ask questions in their native language to get the child to discuss what they read. It is very important that all family members leave believing they can help their child at home no matter what their academic or English skills are.

Activity: Virtual Science Workshop

Purpose: Provide families with ideas of what they can do at home to support their children's learning with commonly available materials.

    Participants: Teacher, families, students, and an interpreter as needed.

    Preparations and resources: Have a short children's book, video, or a chart showing the water cycle. Decide what technology will be used for the workshop. Make sure that families without a computer can participate through their phones. Let families know in advance that they will need a glass filled with ice and a damp cloth.

    Description of activity: Begin by having families fill a glass with ice and dry off the outside of the glass. Also, ask the families to take a wet cloth and wipe it on a table or cutting board so that they can see it is a little wet. Observe these items and then leave them alone until later. Then, explain the water cycle using a book, video, or chart. Next, look at the table or cutting board. Is it drier? Where did the water go? Explain this is a similar process to water from puddles or rivers evaporating and going into the air. Next, have families observe the outside of the glass. Are there water droplets? Let them figure out that the water condensed from the air like it does in the clouds, which are cold like the ice. When water vapor in the air goes high enough, it gets cold and condenses into clouds just like it does on the outside of the glass.

    Options: Similar activities could be done with shadows, leaves, or food webs. Many activities can be done with grocery-store flyers, including math and nutrition activities. Let families know in advance what materials will be needed and try not to require any materials that are uncommon or expensive.

Relevant Literature

The Proudest Blue, by Ibtihaj Muhammad with S. K. Ali (2019), is about a young girl wearing her hijab to school in the United States for the first time. The story is told through the eyes of her little sister who is looking forward to the day she too can wear a blue hijab. Some other students said ugly things to her, but her mother had prepared her. She had told her to be proud and strong. Her mother told her hurtful words "belong only to those who said them." The author was the first U.S. athlete to wear a hijab in the Olympics and the book reflects some of her own life experiences. *Picture book.*

Return to Sender, by Julia Alvarez (2009), is a story told in alternating chapters from the viewpoints of Tyler and Mari, two fifth graders with very different backgrounds, whose lives intersect. Tyler grew up on a dairy farm in Vermont. After Tyler's grandfather dies, his father is crippled in a tractor accident, and his older brother goes to college, they are forced to hire illegal migrant workers or lose the farm. Mari is the daughter of one of the migrant workers and is in the same class at school with Tyler. This is primarily a story of growing friendships across cultures, but it also illuminates the challenges faced by children of illegal immigrants in the United States, which often affects their schooling. They move for better jobs, children have many responsibilities at home, families are often separated, and children may be kept home from school when they fear deportation. *Chapter book.*

References

Auerbach, S. (2009). Walking the walk: Portraits in leadership for family engagement in urban schools. *The School Community Journal*, 19(1), 9–32. https://www.schoolcommunitynetwork.org/SCJ.aspx

Colón, I. T. (2017). *Los recién llegados: Construyendo collaborative relationships between recently arrived Salvadoran parents and educators in the nation's capital.* Dissertation. Loyola University Chicago. https://ecommons.luc.edu/cgi/viewcontent.cgi?article=3789&context=luc_diss

¡Colorín Colorado! (2018). *How to build partnerships with immigrant families.* https://www.colorincolorado.org/immigration/guide/families

Gardner, L. (2019a, November 4). *Immigrant and English learner parent advocacy.* Immigrant Connections. https://www.immigrantsrefugeesandschools.org/post/immigrant-and-english-learner-parent-advocacy

Gardner, L. (2019b, February, 14). *Separate or together: Unpacking the "EL family event" vs. "all-school family event" debate.* Immigrant Connections. https://www.immigrantsrefugeesandschools.org/post/separate-or-together-unpacking-the-el-family-event-vs-all-school-family-event-debate

Han, Y.-c. & Love, J. (2015). Stages of immigrant parent involvement - Survivors to leaders. *Phi Delta Kappan*, 97(4), 21–25. https://doi.org/10.1177/0031721715619913

Knackendoffel, A., Dettmer, P., & Thurston, L. P. (2017). *Collaboration, consultation, and teamwork for students with special needs* (8th ed.). Pearson.

Lazarín, M. (2020, June). *COVID-19 spotlights the inequities facing English learner students as nonprofit organizations seek to mitigate challenges.* Migration

Policy Institute. https://www.migrationpolicy.org/news/covid-19-inequities-english-learner-students

Mexican American Legal Defense and Educational Fund & National Education Association. (2010, June). *Minority parent and community engagement: Best practices and policy recommendations for closing the gaps in student achievement.* http://www.parentcenterhub.org/wp-content/uploads/2016/09/Minority-Parent-and-Community-Engagement_maldef-report_final.pdf

Muhammad, I. & Ali, S. K. (2019). *The Proudest Blue.* Little, Brown Books for Young Readers.

National Association of Elementary School Principals, 2008. *Leading learning communities: Standards for what principals should know and be able to do* (2nd ed.). Collaborative Communications Group. https://www.naesp.org/sites/default/files/resources/1/Pdfs/LLC2-ES.pdf

Parent Teacher Association, (2010, August 4). *Advocacy training-full training manual.* National PTA. https://www.pta.org/home/advocacy/advocacy-resources/Advocacy-Toolkit/Advocacy-Training-Full-Training-Manual

Williamson, R. & Blackburn, B. (2016, April 17). Principals: Teaming with family & community. *Middleweb.* https://www.middleweb.com/29369/principals-teaming-with-families-community/

7

Partnering with Families of Students with Special Needs

Scenario: Active Child

Markos was a handful. Rosemary knew it. As a mother, she knew he was very active and very compulsive. The children's birthday parties she attended with Markos almost always ended with him grabbing a piece out of the birthday cake or with the birthday child's new toy broken in pieces. He wasn't hurtful or malicious; he just was into everything. In fact, his joy was infectious. He waved at all the neighbors and called out to them when they walked by.

Rosemary's husband was about 20 years older than she was, with grand-children from his first marriage. He either let Markos run wild without comment or punished him with a belt if something especially important was broken. At home with Rosemary, Markos was a doll; he was always making a funny face to make her laugh. He also was quick with "Lo siento" or I'm sorry, one of the first phases he learned in his childcare settings. It was impossible not to forgive him right away.

Rosemary had a medical degree from Mexico where she had practiced for a few years before coming to the United States. In the United States, her degree was not considered sufficient, so she had to find work as a nurse. She was especially invaluable as she could translate for the doctors and was able to make suggestions for treatments. Despite her training, she was not quite ready when the assistant principal at Markos' school called and said they needed to set up an appointment to discuss referring Markos for assessments. The teachers at the school thought he might have attention deficit hyperactivity disorder (ADHD) and that he might need medication to stay focused at school.

Rosemary was devastated because she felt it might somehow be her fault. Although she was highly educated and spoke English fairly fluently, she had difficulty taking in all of the jargon used in her first meeting with the diagnostician. She signed the papers to allow testing, but she had some misgivings. She had the feeling that if they just let him move around a bit more and did not expect him to sit so long that he would be able to adjust to kindergarten. But she kept her mouth shut, feeling that the experts should be the ones to decide.

The process of determining whether a child has disabilities or special needs is difficult for both the school and the family. Having a child diagnosed with special needs can be devastating. It can also be confusing as it involves both an educational and legal process. This can be especially difficult for families who are not proficient in English.

Language and Culture

The referral process for children who are emergent bilinguals requires that the designation of the disability not be based on linguistic or cultural differences. Despite this requirement, emergent bilinguals are disproportionately referred to special education. Students who are incorrectly placed into special education programs may not receive the language support they need, fall further behind, and miss out on academic opportunities for the rest of their school career (Robertson et al., n.d.) For emergent bilinguals with special needs, it is often difficult to get appropriate support for both language and disabilities, partially because bilingual and special education departments often do not communicate well.

Under-referring special needs can be a problem too. Students who need extra help and don't receive it can suffer academically. Early intervention has been shown to be important for the long-term success of students with true underlying disabilities (Sutterby & Young, 2020).

Correct identification can be difficult with immigrant students. For example, a natural response for a young child being placed in an environment where no one speaks his or her language is to enter a silent period. This unresponsiveness might be identified as a sign of a child with autism (Guiberson, 2009). Cultural differences also can result in misidentification. For example, there was a student who was constantly getting out of his seat, which the teacher perceived as hyperactivity. However, the parent revealed that he was getting out of his seat to help the teacher, which was something that was done to please the teacher in his culture (Hess, 2017). Instead of asking whether students are struggling due to language, culture, or disability, Robertson et al. (n.d.) recommend asking: "What are the student's needs and how are they being met?" (p. 2).

Families Sharing Important Information

In order to reduce unnecessary referrals, schools should work with families to better understand the child and the family context. This is especially important for recent immigrant families who may not have previous education records. Families can fill in some of the gaps. For example, have the children previously gone to school? Where? Were they in native language, English as a second language (ESL), bilingual, dual language, or English only programs? Did the child have any learning difficulties in previous schools? Is the child exposed to any English at home? (i.e., TV, older sibling, other relative). Professional interpretation is extremely important for these sensitive meetings. For example, Robertson et al. (n.d.) explain there is no term for "special education" in the Somali language. "If the interpretation is not done sensitively, the family may believe the staff is referring to the student as 'crazy' or 'mentally defective'" (p. 7).

In addition to learning about the student's and family's history, educators should ask families about their observations at home. Is the child quiet at home like at school? Does the child have trouble sitting still at home or just at school?

Some children spend part of the week or school year with one family member and part with another family member. It is important to provide both custodial family members with opportunities to communicate with the school. This will provide the school with more information and encourage continuity in messages to the student.

Accommodations in the Inclusive Classroom

For the remainder of the chapter, any non-special education classroom will be referred to as an inclusive classroom even if it is a bilingual, dual language, or an ESL class.

When teachers or families notice a child struggling in school, they usually should begin by making accommodations in the inclusive classroom.

Table 7.1 Accommodations and Modifications

Accommodations	Modifications
Accommodations help a student overcome a disability by changing **how** the student learns or shows mastery of something. Standards and expectations stay the same, but the student is allowed to do them differently.	Modification refers to changes in **what** the student is to learn. The standards and expectations are different from peers.

Although the law does not require educators to involve families in these accommodations, families often have insights that will assist teachers. In addition, families who are involved will better understand requests for further measures if necessary (Table 7.1).

For example, Lindsay is having a hard time paying attention when the teacher is speaking to the whole class but has little trouble in one-to-one situations. Ms. Kucherlapati shares this information with the family and learns that Lindsay has had repeated ear infections and might have trouble hearing. Rather than pursuing the attention problem, the teacher can now work with the school nurse about possible hearing loss.

Pedro was constantly fidgeting at school. When Ms. Miller talked to his father, Ben, she learned they had fidget toys at home that Pedro used when he needed to stay still. Ben said he didn't want Pedro to get in trouble for bringing a toy to school but would be happy to send one to school with him. Ms. Miller thanked him for his consideration and asked him to send the toy with Pedro. The next day Ms. Miller explained to the class that Pedro had brought something to school that helped him learn better just like other students had glasses that helped them see better. The novelty soon wore off, and Pedro benefited from this accommodation.

In another case, Angela, a first grader in a bilingual class, didn't seem interested in reading in either English or Spanish, her native language. Her teacher Mr. Sanchez learned that Angela's parents said a lullaby to her every night before bed in Spanish. They were happy to write the lullaby down for Mr. Sanchez. Angela was excited to learn to read the lullaby herself and after learning to read it successfully became interested in reading other things.

Before making referrals for special education, Robertson et al. (n.d.) recommend asking whether the disability is present in the home language as well as English. If it is only present in English, then the problem most likely stems from lack of English proficiency and further language support should be provided. Observers also should remember that social language develops before academic language.

Assessments

When there is not appropriate growth in the inclusive classroom from accommodations, educators and families may decide to do additional assessments to determine or identify special needs either under Section 504 of the Rehabilitation Act of 1973 or special education under the Individuals with Disabilities Education Act (IDEA, https://sites.ed.gov/idea/about-idea/). Both laws require that students with disabilities receive a free and appropriate education comparable to the education received by students without disabilities. Section 504 requires parental notification and IDEA requires parental consent, but parental consent is recommended for both processes (Mitchell & Edmonson, 2020).

Despite the need for evaluation to identify special needs, assessments can be tricky with emergent bilinguals. Standardized assessments may be one of the reasons for over representation of emergent bilinguals in special education. Even when standardized assessments are translated into the home language, they may not be appropriate because the tests were normed with populations that do not match the culture and language of the child being tested (Fletcher & Navarrete, 2011). The following story exemplifies how difficult it can be to accurately access an emergent bilingual.

Scenario: Assessment Difficulties

Margarita had been a teacher in Guatemala but was still working on her English and getting a teacher certificate in the United States. The school had asked Margarita to allow them to assess her daughter Carolina for reading difficulties. Now, she was going to the school to discuss the results of the assessments. Margarita really didn't think her daughter, Carolina, had a reading problem but she wanted to hear what the school had to say.

When Margarita arrived, the committee explained assessment results showing that her child had reading problems in English. The psychologist said Carolina had been asked to read aloud and then answer questions about the text. She had also been given an oral fluency assessment in which her oral reading speed and errors were measured. Margarita learned that no silent-reading assessment had been conducted. She explained to the committee that Carolina had been bullied, was extremely self-conscious of her accent, and couldn't concentrate on meaning when asked to read aloud. She asked that a silent-reading assessment be done before any decisions were made. The school staff apologized and said they were not aware of the child's bullying. The scenario shows the importance of involving families early in the process, using assessments that are appropriate for culturally and linguistically diverse children, and collecting a variety of different types of information.

Sutterby and Young (2020) believe that bias in assessment should always be considered to avoid over-referring children whose "academic delays are due to cultural and linguistic differences rather than an underlying disability" (p. 132). Less formal assessments such as observations in multiple settings and work samples may provide a better picture of the child's strengths and needs.

Individualized Education Plan (IEP) Meetings

When families agree to assessments and assessment results indicate one or more of the 13 disabilities under IDEA, families meet with a committee of inclusive and special education teachers, an administrator, and the specialist(s) who administered the assessments to design an IEP for their child. Collaboration between families and the school can be encouraged with pre-meeting planning that involves all stakeholders, including families (Diliberto & Brewer, 2014; Knackendoffel et al., 2017). The specialists recommend sharing assessment results at least two weeks before the formal IEP meeting. This allows families time to talk to friends and family or do research before being asked to make decisions that may affect the rest of their child's life. All stakeholders should be informed of what the assessment means for the student's success now and in the future. The law requires that information and meetings are in the language requested by the family (Wright, 2016).

For the most appropriate education services, the school should provide the family with resources that will help them better understand the assessments and the diagnoses. IDEA funds Parent Training and Information Centers in every state which offer special education training and advocacy (in multiple languages) at no cost to families. Information about the centers as well as related resources can be found at the Center for Parent Information and Resources.

¡Colorín Colorado! has articles in English and Spanish such as one titled: *10 steps for parents if your child has a learning disability (n.d.).* Wrightslaw Way (2019) provides advocacy tips online to help families make long-term plans with the school for the most appropriate education for their child (see *Special Needs Resources Activity* below).

Some families prefer their privacy, but other families may be interested in the support provided by Parent to Parent USA (https://www.p2pusa. org/parents). This is a free program that matches trained and experienced families with those seeking information or emotional support. The matches are based on the child's special needs and the families' locations and situations. Some matches simply provide information and short-term support, while others last for years as the children in both families go through different stages of life.

School districts have special education procedural safeguard manuals describing the educational and legal procedures associated with special education, but even when the information is translated, it often means little to immigrant families who are not familiar with schooling in the United States or the jargon used in the manuals. Therefore, it is important to provide families with information before IEP meetings in their native language and in language without jargon (Table 7.2).

When families are involved from the beginning of the process, they will better understand when further intervention is necessary for their child to progress. Families may respect teachers as experts on the educational process, but what many families value more than anything is the caring relationship that the teacher demonstrates toward the child and the openness to communication with the family. Although family members do not necessarily see themselves as experts in the area of special education, they do express a desire to know what is going on and why (Hess et al., 2006).

Schools need to respect student and family privacy, but it is important that all school personnel who have contact with the student know there is an

Table 7.2 Pre-IEP Meeting Checklist for Families

- What issues have been observed at school?
- How does this impact my child's learning?
- What steps has the school already taken?
- What alternatives are available now?
- What does the school believe should be done and why?
- What are all the impacts? For example, if my child needs help with reading, will he/she be able to read enough for social studies and science in the inclusive classroom?
- What if this doesn't work? When can the plan be changed by the parent, student, or school?
- What are the long-term impacts on the child's life?
- Will my child receive extra services through 12th grade? Will he/she be eligible for a regular diploma?
- What are long-term realistic goals for my child?
- Will my child truly be able to participate in academic activities in the inclusive classroom in a meaningful way?
- Where can I get additional information?
- How is an IEP meeting conducted?
- Who can I bring with me to the IEP meeting?

individual plan in place and how to get more details if needed, especially if there are behavioral implications.

Student Involvement in IEPs

Students must be involved in IEP meetings about post-high school transitions, but student advocacy and student voice should start as early as possible according to Elizabeth Campos Hamilton, Region III Director of the Learning Disabilities Association of Illinois (personal communication, November 9, 2020). The decisions made in IEP meetings impact the rest of the student's life, not just his education. The video *The Best Me I Can Be* (DCEducation, 2013) provides guidance and encouragement for student IEP involvement, which can vary from observation to leading the meeting.

Teachers can meet with students in advance of the meeting to choose work samples and other indications of progress as well as discussing future goals. If an interpreter is needed, neither the student nor a family member should serve in that role. Knackendoffel et al. (2017) say teachers, families, and students learn from these experiences.

On-Going Communication

It is always important to learn more about families' needs, but it is especially vital for families of emergent bilinguals with special needs. IDEA requires that IEP meetings are conducted at least once a year and that families receive a new copy of the special education procedural safeguards, but meetings can be held more often to assure the student is receiving an appropriate education and that the school and family are communicating similar messages to the student.

One school reached out to Spanish-speaking parents who attended IEP meetings at the district's high school. At the end of each IEP meeting held, a survey was distributed in Spanish to parents asking them what information or topic they would like to learn more about related to special education and their child's needs. For three months, survey data were gathered at the end of the IEP meetings. At the end of the three months, the survey results revealed that parents wanted more information about transitions. Parents were concerned how their children would transition from high school to work or college. Based on the results, the high school gathered materials in Spanish and prepared a presentation for Spanish-speaking parents about the issue of transitions, which were of great interest and concern to families.

Although this activity was conducted in Spanish, it could easily be modified to fit the linguistic needs of other families. Additionally, it should be noted that the survey was administered orally in Spanish to those parents who were not comfortable answering the survey in writing. This practice showed sensitivity to the literacy levels of the families.

The survey and follow-up meeting communicated to parents that the school was interested in helping them learn more about special education and was available to answer questions and provide additional information as needed. It is also an example of how a needs assessment can be targeted to a portion of parents who may have a specific need for specialized information. This experience underscores that the school cannot make assumptions that families are familiar with special education issues and practices when no questions are raised. Parents may feel intimidated by the group of highly educated professionals to whom they trust their children and not want to ask questions in front of a large group.

Individualizing for Families

Cultural Beliefs about Special Needs

Communication with families about a child's special needs should be individualized to respect their strengths, beliefs, and needs. Beliefs about special needs vary among cultures (Caring for Kids New to Canada, n.d.). Some families may believe a child having a disability is their fault due to a problem during pregnancy or as punishment for something they did wrong. Other families may believe they received a special needs child because they were the ones most capable of taking care of the child. Some believe that the child will grow out of any delays while others actively seek help from the school. Teachers need to be sensitive to these beliefs and be especially careful of saying things that may be perceived as blaming the family for the special needs. Educators also should be aware of their own beliefs and have high expectations for all students.

Stress from Special Needs

In addition to being sensitive to cultural issues, teachers should understand that some special needs children place families under additional stress. Having a child with disabilities may place the family under extra economic strain due to medical bills and extra care. Children with special needs may require extra attention, which can cause conflicts with siblings who feel they are being ignored.

Family Members with Special Needs

The law also requires that special accommodations be made for families with special needs to participate in their children's education. For example, a parent who has profound hearing loss may need to communicate with the school through texts or emails. A note should be placed next to the student's name so that no one in the school calls or leaves voice messages on the parent's phone.

Gifted and Talented Programs

While emergent bilinguals are overrepresented in some special needs programs, they are underrepresented in programs for gifted children according to the National Association for Gifted Children. One of the biggest factors is trying to identify gifted learners who come from different cultures and language backgrounds. According to the association, emergent bilinguals should be identified at the same time the rest of the population is screened for gifted programs, but many schools wait for English skills to develop. According to the association, it takes three to five years for students to develop oral English proficiency and an understanding of the culture and four to seven years for students to become proficient in English. "Waiting for students to develop oral and academic English proficiency, then, would cause GT (Gifted Talented) emergent bilinguals to lose years of potential opportunities for further growth" (Langley, 2016, p. 2). Students who are not challenged may become bored and tune out or act up.

Langley (2016) recommends two approaches to identify emergent bilinguals who are gifted. The first involves using a variety of assessment tools, including culturally sensitive standardized assessments, such as the Torrance Tests of Creative Thinking (https://www.ststesting.com/gift/), as well as informal assessments, such as observations, student interviews, and work samples. The second approach involves providing students with more gifted curriculum in the inclusive classroom. This would include critical thinking, creativity, and problem-solving activities that would nurture talents that could be formally assessed when the student had higher levels of English proficiency. Knackendoffel et al. (2017) recommend allowing potential gifted students to skip repetitive material, work at a flexible pace, and have opportunities to do self-directed projects.

Bullying

Unfortunately, students with special needs and English learners (ELs) are at greater risk for being bullied. "Any number of factors—physical vulnerability, social skill challenges, or intolerant environments—may increase the risk" (stopbullying.gov, 2018, p. 1). The consequences of being bullied, bullying, or even witnessing bullying can be serious and life-long. They include depression, anxiety, poor grades, and lack of self-confidence. Teachers and families need to work together to identify and resolve bullying issues. Many times, the student doesn't share the bullying with adults. If it occurs in places such as cafeterias, buses, bathrooms, or online, teachers and families may not observe the bullying. Families and teachers need to watch for changes in behavior such as loss of appetite, less interest in activities, changes in friends, or changes in online behavior.

If either the teacher or family believe bullying is occurring, they should work together to resolve the problem. It is important to get as much information as possible about what is happening, who is involved, and where it is occurring. Provide emotional support for the child and explain that it is not their fault. Do not encourage the student to fight back or get revenge.

Peer support seems to be one of the most important factors in reducing bullying (stopbullying.gov, 2018). The teacher and family can work together to involve the child in more group activities where they can be successful. This might be sports, music, or art classes with peers. The teacher can do team building activities in the classroom in which each person has an assigned role that makes them successful. One high school established a lunch program for students with special needs and those without to eat together. Several seniors led the group. Many of the students formed friendships that extended beyond lunchtime (see *Bullying Role Playing Activity* at the end of chapter).

If additional help is needed, such as counseling, the school may need to call a meeting to revise the student's 504 plan or IEP. The committee, including families, may also come up with other accommodations that would reduce the bullying and help the student with social interactions. There are many reasons to take bullying seriously including civil rights laws that protect people with disabilities from harm. Schools that are having widespread bullying problems should consider adopting initiatives that promote belonging. Also, see the *Talking to Children about Diversity Activity* in Chapter 8.

The following activities are designed to improve teacher communication with immigrant families of special needs students. Families also may be empowered with the information and contacts provided in the *Special Education Resources Activity* and through skills learned and practiced in the *Bullying Role Playing Activity*.

Activity: Bullying Role Playing

Purpose: To reduce bullying and build family and school relationships. Immigrant students and students with special needs are at increased risk for bullying.

Participants: This activity can be conducted with educators only, families only, older students only, or a mixture of participants. Interpreter(s).

Preparation and resources: Invite participants. Day care should be provided, or families should be discouraged from bringing young children who may not understand role playing and be frightened by the activity. Prepare some scenarios in advance that are appropriate for the age and special needs of the children. Have the scenarios translated into appropriate home languages.

Description of activity: Explain the purpose of the activity. Families from some cultures may not be familiar with role-playing. The interpreter should make sure they understand that this is not about their family but helps prepare them if something like this should happen. The teachers and an experienced family member may want to do a scenario first. Break into groups of four by language if possible. One person will be the student, another a parent, the third a teacher, and the fourth a discussion leader. Allow the participants to choose their roles but encourage them to switch after the first scenario.

Sample Scenario

Student: The teacher said the class could play some games if everyone finished our work early, but I didn't understand the work. The whole class was waiting for me to finish. When we went to lunch, the other kids said it was all my fault they didn't get to play.

Parent: Parent responds to child (role play).

Parent or parent and student: Go to school to talk to the teacher (role play).

Teacher: Responds to parent (and student). Parent and teacher (and student) come up with a plan (role play).

Discussion leader: How did you think it went? What else could they have done?

Options: Have older students or family members come up with scenarios for the role playing. Do this activity first with teachers only to see how the scenarios work and to work on some possible solutions in case the families get stuck.

Activity: Special Needs Resources

Purpose: To collect sources of information about special needs in a variety of languages. The goal is to have an online database of organizations and sources of information in a variety of languages. This database should be easily accessible to teachers and families. An individual teacher may only need information about dyslexia in Arabic once in her career but many teachers in the district may need it at some time.

Participant: A district-wide employee responsible for creating and updating the database.

Description of activity: Someone familiar with special needs in the district would be hired to create a database that would include websites and community organizations that provide information and assistance for various special needs. For each entry, there would be an outline of the information and/or services provided and the availability of languages other than English. Once the database was created, teachers could submit additions and updates to a central person who would enter them on the database. Since websites and organizations change frequently, it is important to keep the database up to date.

Options: Gather ideas from families for the database. The district may want to include appropriate children's and young adult literature on the list with brief descriptions.

Relevant Literature

Just Ask: Be Different, Be Brave, Be You, by Sonia Sotomayor and illustrated by Rafael Lopez (2019), is about children who may be viewed as different. Sotomayor, the supreme court justice, has had diabetes since childhood and was aware she was different from other children. She describes 12 different children and ways of being in the book. Sotomayor compares these children to different plants in a garden, each contributing something special. *Picture book.*

The Spirit Catches You and You Fall Down, by Anne Fadiman (1998), is the true story of a Hmong family with a child with epilepsy. The story focuses on the difficulties the medical system has interacting with the family. The Hmong family viewed the seizures as a spiritual experience rather than as a disability. The medical system wanted the family to conform to the drug regimen, but the family did not see the value of the medications. This provides a good example of how people from other cultures may view things differently leading to confusion of the roles of families and schools. This book has become an important text used in training medical staff in many programs. *Chapter book.*

References

Caring for Kids New to Canada. (n.d.). *Development disabilities across cultures*. https://www.kidsnewtocanada.ca/mental-health/developmental-disability

Center for Parent Information & Resources. (2017, June 6). *About specific disabilities.* https://www.parentcenterhub.org/specific-disabilities/

¡Colorín Colorado! (n.d.). *10 steps for parents: If your child has a learning disability.* https://www.colorincolorado.org/article/10-steps-parents-if-your-child-has-learning-disability

DCEducation. (2013, December 13). *The best me I can be: Module 1.* [Video] You Tube. https://www.youtube.com/watch?v=aRWvu-Jovs8&feature=emb_logo

Diliberto, J. A. & Brewer, D. (2014). Six tips for successful IEP meetings. *Teaching Exceptional Children,* 47(2), 128–135. https://doi.org/10.1177/0040059914553205

Fletcher, T. V. & Navarrete, L. A. (2011). Learning disabilities or difference: A critical look at issues associated with the misidentification and placement of Hispanic students in special education programs. *Rural Special Education Quarterly,* 30(1), 30–38. https://doi.org/10.1177/875687051103000106

Guiberson, M. (2009). Hispanic representation in special education: Patterns and implications. *Preventing School Failure: Alternative Education for Children and Youth,* 53(3), 167–176. https://doi.org/10.3200/PSFL.53.3.167-176

Hess, R. (2017). *Social and emotional support for refugee families: A school psychology perspective.* ¡Colorín Colorado! https://www.colorincolorado.org/article/social-and-emotional-support-refugee-families-school-psychology-perspective

Hess, R., Molina, A., & Kozleski, E. (2006). Until somebody hears me: Parent voice and advocacy in special education decision making. *British Journal of Special Education,* 33(3), 148–157. https://doi.org/10.1111/j.1467-8578.2006.00430.x

Knackendoffel, A., Dettmer, P., & Thurston, L. P. (2017). *Collaboration, consultation, and teamwork for students with special needs* (8th ed.). Pearson.

Langley, S. D. (2016, February 10). *Fostering equitable access to gifted services for English learners through a balance of measures and program options.* National Association for Gifted Children. https://www.nagc.org/blog/fostering-equitable-access-gifted-services-english-learners-through-balance-measures-and

Mitchell, V. J. & Edmonson, S. I. (2020). Special education. In Pankake, A., Abrego, J., & Abrego, M. (Eds.) *The administration and supervision of special programs in education* (4th ed.) Kendall Hunt Publisher, 25–46.

Robertson, K., Sanchez-Lopez, C., & Breiseth, L. (n.d.). *Addressing ELLs' language learning and special education needs: Questions and considerations.* ¡Colorín Colorado! https://www.colorincolorado.org/article/addressing-ells-language-learning-and-special-education-needs-questions-and-considerations

stopbullying.gov. (2018, July 23). *Bullying and youth with disabilities and special health needs.* https://www.stopbullying.gov/bullying/special-needs

Sutterby, J. A. & Young, V. J. (2020). Early childhood program for children with special needs. In Pankake, A., Abrego, J., & Abrego, M. (Eds.) *The administration and supervision of special programs in education* (4th ed.) Kendall Hunt Publisher, 125–138.

Wright, P. (2016, September 8). *Ensuring meaningful communication with parents who have limited English proficiency.* The Wrightslaw Way. https://www.wrightslaw.com/blog/ensuring-meaningful-communication-with-parents-who-have-limited-english-proficiency/

Wrightslaw. (2019, October 17). *Effective advocacy – 4 mistakes parents make.* The Wrightslaw Way. https://www.wrightslaw.com/blog/effective-advocacy-4-mistakes-parents-make/

8

Immigrant Families under Stress

Scenario: New Students

Ms. Johnson, the school secretary, has admitted six new children during the third week of November at Brunswick Elementary. For Ms. Johnson, this is an especially large number of new enrollments at this time of year. Normally, she might admit one or two students per month after school started at the elementary campus. Surprised by the large number, she brings it to the attention of Mr. Baldwin, the school principal.

Mr. Baldwin does not seem surprised by the news. He mentions that in the last election, Sheriff James from Jefferson County won the election with the slogan, "Every traffic stop will require documentation." "I suspected that some of the families from Jefferson County would relocate over here," Principal Baldwin explained to Ms. Johnson.

> *Please try to set up a meeting with the new parents ASAP. I want them to know that they are welcome at our school and that to the best of our ability they will be safe here at Brunswick Elementary.*

Sources of Stress and Trauma

Principals, such as Baldwin above, realize that many immigrant families need extra support. They may have suffered trauma both before and after arriving in the United States. They may have witnessed war, killing of relatives in front of them, refugee camps, lack of food and water, and/or long arduous trips to get to the United States. Even after arriving in the United States, they may have experienced trauma. Some families were separated at the border. Others live in constant fear that someone in the family will be deported. Families who were pillars of their home communities and forced to move by war or persecution may now be reduced to poverty and desperation. The pandemic hit low-income families harder than other families in terms of health and economic security. Both immigrant students and families are often the targets of racism, prejudice, and bullying. Schools, which often provide stability for immigrant children with everything from academic content to after school care to school meals, were closed for months during the pandemic.

The pandemic made clear that schools play many roles in addition to instruction (Samuels, 2020). One of the major roles is providing healthy meals to students (No Kid Hungry, 2020). In addition, schools realized that social–emotional learning often needed to occur before traditional academic learning could be successful (Gross, 2020). In order to better understand these demands, some school districts referred to Maslow's Hierarchy of Needs, which was developed to describe what needs should be satisfied before people can reach their full potential (Maslow, 1943/2000). The hierarchy provides a useful tool but should not replace open communication with families, nor should assumptions be made about where families are along this continuum. Families also may jump back and forth among the levels depending on the situation. It does help educators better understand and have empathy for families under stress, who may not be ready to fully participate in the education system. The wording used in this book may be slightly different from the original description of the hierarchy of needs, but the ideas presented here reflect the original intention of Maslow.

Hierarchy of Needs

Food and Shelter

The first level of the hierarchy is food, water, and shelter. More than half of the students in public schools were eligible for free or reduced-priced lunches based on their families' income in the 2016–2017 school year. Immigrant families are more likely to experience poverty even though employment rates are higher among immigrants than persons born in the United States (Bureau of Labor Statistics, 2020). Immigrants generally work more hours, have lower wage jobs, and are less likely to receive government assistance. We usually don't think of homelessness impacting children, yet over 1.5 million children attending public schools in the 2017–2018 school year (pre-k-12) were homeless (National Center for Homeless Education, 2019).

In addition to the free and reduced meal programs at schools, educators can help connect families with community and faith-based organizations that may be able to help them with food and housing (see *Community Resources Activity* below). For example, Swansboro High School in North Carolina partnered with the mayor's office and local churches to find volunteers to take meals to families without transportation during the pandemic (Gross, 2020). They worked with Backpack Buddies, which is sponsored by Feeding America and local organizations, to provide food over the weekend.

Safety and Security

Safety and security are Maslow's second level of needs (Maslow, 1943/2000). Schools should collaborate with all families on identifying and resolving as many safety issues concerning the school as possible (see *School Safety Survey Activity* in Chapter 3). Many issues may be nearly invisible to educators because they occur at the bus stop, bathroom, or at other times when educators are not observing.

In addition to these general safety needs, immigrants face special issues. One in four children in U.S. public schools live with at least one immigrant parent. Most students of immigrant families are U.S.-born citizens, but about 4.5 million children have at least one undocumented parent (Urban Institute, 2019). Undocumented families have been targeted politically and legally. This can have a profound impact on children who are U.S. citizens but who have undocumented family members. "These children and youth are important to the nation's future, but their development and well-being are at considerable risk from harmful federal policy changes and the pervasive climate of fear these have engendered" (Yoshikawa et al., 2019, p. 1).

Even though teachers are usually not aware of families' residency status and cannot legally ask about their status, it still may impact families' interactions with the school. Family members may avoid participating in school field trips and sporting events. Undocumented parents often encourage children to remain close to home, and they avoid as much contact as possible with what they perceive as government agencies, including schools, medical care, and social services. It is especially important to have several emergency contacts for immigrant families so the child can leave school with someone they know if a parent is detained or deported. Schools also should have information about legal aid available for immigrant families included in its community resources list.

Relationships and Belonging

Maslow's third level in the hierarchy is building relationships and a sense of belonging (Maslow, 1943/2000). This process is difficult for immigrant students and families because they are new to the culture and often its language. In addition, they frequently face racism and prejudice. Overt and more subtle racism and prejudice have been growing in the United States, and immigrants are often the target. Black, Muslim, Hispanic, Asian American, and other immigrants have all been subjects of discrimination both in and outside of school (Table 8.1).

Personal Discrimination

Personal discrimination occurs among students, families, and school staff. This may involve prejudice based on skin color or lack of patience as the student or family member tries to express themselves in English. We often think of bullying as something that just occurs between students, but 25 percent of cases of bullying of Muslims reported in 2017 involved teachers and administrators (Ochieng, 2017). "Children who receive negative messages about themselves at school may be less likely to achieve academic success, graduate from school, and ultimately, surpass their parents' economic position" (Adair, 2015, p. 4).

Structural Discrimination

In addition to these personal issues, immigrants also face structural discrimination in the education system. More than half the students in the United States attend schools that are majority people of color or majority white (EdBuild, n.d.). Most immigrants are students of color. The schools that are majority students of color are funded at $23 billion a year less than those serving mostly white students, or $2,226 per student less (EdBuild). This means there are fewer academically challenging courses, less experienced teachers,

Table 8.1 Racism, Prejudice, and Discrimination as Used in this Book

Racism	Prejudice	Personal Discrimination	Structural Discrimination
Attaching negative characteristics to individuals based on their memberships in a specific race rather than their individual achievements.	Prejudice is prejudging people based on non-race factors, such as gender or accents.	Discrimination is unfair practices based on racism or prejudice. Personal discrimination is between individuals, such as harsher discipline for immigrant students.	Discrimination may be a part of the system, such as lower funding for schools that have mostly students of color.

and fewer after-school activities. These schools have higher rates of suspension and expulsion too (Scott et al., 2017). School funding rates impact society as a whole through job preparation, welfare rates, and crime (Raikes & Darling-Hammond, 2019).

Family Discrimination

Immigrant parents also feel the impact of racism and prejudice at school. Teachers and administrators may wrongly assume immigrant families can't contribute to their children's education. The families themselves may be aware of negative feelings toward immigrant families and, therefore, may limit interaction with the school (Adair, 2015).

Reducing Discrimination

Considering these feelings, it is even more important for schools to create a welcoming environment (see Chapter 3). Creating strong reciprocal relationships with families is the Migration Policy Institute's number one suggestion for fighting racism and discrimination in the schools (Adair, 2015). Ideas for creating more equal partnerships with immigrant families are found in all chapters of our book (Table 8.2).

One of the best ways to reduce racism and prejudice is for people to get to know each other on a personal level rather than thinking of them as one homogenous group. Along the Texas–Mexico border, Hispanic families often invite teachers of all backgrounds to their homes for birthday parties and other events. Teachers consider it an honor to be invited, and families feel honored if the teacher attends. It is an excellent way for them to get to know one another and for teachers to see and appreciate students in their home culture. If such opportunities are not available near you, it is still possible to go to neighborhood events, restaurants, or markets in areas where your students live (see *New Teacher Induction/Community Travel Activity* in Chapter 3).

Immigrant Connections offers local cultural immersion courses that include general cultural awareness activities, interviews of local immigrants, observations, and field trips into the local community, including homes and places of worship. The purpose of these courses is to reduce cultural gaps between families and educators, thereby facilitating student achievement.

Table 8.2 Ways to Reduce Discrimination

> - Recognize that families are experts about their own children.
> - Find out what immigrant families need and want.
> - Respect the knowledge, languages, and abilities of immigrant families.
> - Partner with them for student success.
> - Involve diverse families and community members in decision-making.

Home visits are another way to get to know families better on an individual basis (Sheldon & Jung, 2015). One middle school teacher who participated in a home visit program in Sacramento, California, wrote this on the program's website.

> *I thought I'm black, you're black, so we have an automatic connection, but that wasn't necessarily the case. I represented an institution that they, the families, didn't trust. I'm educated, I'm a teacher and I'm part of a system that hasn't treated them very well. So, I still had to work hard to bridge the gap. I tried everything, but it wasn't until Parent Teacher Home Visits (http://www.pthvp.org/) that I was able to change the dynamics.*
>
> (See more about home visits in Chapter 4)

Discussions about racism are uncomfortable, especially with people you don't know well, but experts say these discussions are important to breaking down barriers (Matisak, 2020). Children's books, poetry, and short videos are great discussion starters for both adults and children. Have interpreters to make discussions available to families in their preferred languages. The *Talking to Children about Diversity Activity* at the end of the chapter is one example of how families can interact and prepare to talk to their children about diversity and racism.

Finally, self-reflection about racism, prejudice, and discrimination is more important now than ever before. Although about 79 percent of teachers in the United States are white (National Center for Education Statistics, 2020a), approximately 52 percent of students are from some minority group (National Center for Education Statistics, 2020b). Gorski (2019) emphasizes that teachers and schools need to be careful not to shift responsibility for reducing racism onto students and families, who are not the ones in power. He suggests examining policies such as tracking and behavior guidelines to see if some of these are leading to different outcomes for students of color. In addition, staff members, including school security or resource officers, can ask themselves questions such as: In what ways can I better reach out to immigrant families and build partnerships with them? What beliefs do I have about groups that may influence the way I respond to specific students or families? (See the *Questioning Prejudices Activity* below.)

Self-Esteem and Accomplishment

Maslow's fourth level in the hierarchy is self-esteem and accomplishment (Maslow, 1943/2000). Understandably, immigrant students who have suffered trauma, live in poverty, or experience discrimination and other hardships may have trouble focusing on school. Families may be frustrated because they cannot support their families in the same way they did in their home countries due to lack of education, English-language skills, residency status, or lack of U.S. certifications in their fields, such as nursing.

Beginning in the 2016–2017 school year, Santa Cruz, California saw an increase in Salvadoran students, whose stories reflect many U.S. immigrants who are escaping violence in their home countries. Robles (2018), a social worker, shared what she had learned from the students and their families. She said unusual student behavior is often misinterpreted as defiance when it is really caused by trauma. Robles said, "…the behavior of these students cannot be interpreted in the same way as other non-traumatized students" (p. 9). For example, many immigrant students may understand a discussion but choose not to participate because they don't want to reveal personal information.

The school district quickly realized that they needed extra help and received a grant from the City of Santa Cruz to provide support from two therapists. One therapist, who conducted group and individual counseling for families at one of the schools, came from the Salvadoran immigrant community herself, which helped her understand the language and culture. When dealing with mental health issues, it is important to be sensitive to cultural issues (Gardner, 2019). The typical medical model of intervention in which an individual is asked to talk through and relive their trauma with a stranger often makes the problem worse.

The social workers and therapists were able to share information with the families and the students' teachers about how the students' traumatic experiences might affect them in and outside of school. In addition, they began to realize what students needed to feel safe and accepted at school. The therapists and social workers also learned from the families. They learned about the resilience of the families and their desire to succeed in the United States, including learning English.

Robles (2018) provided some advice for other schools working with new groups of immigrants. She said teachers should not pity these students but rather feel empathy. Although teachers are usually caring people who want to help, Robles advised them to contact mental health professionals to support their students' well-being.

Language is also important. Although Robles (2018) spoke Spanish and so did the Salvadoran families, they used different vocabulary. She says she constantly checked to make sure they were fully understanding each other and that she wasn't accidentally insulting them. Robles also said partnerships with various community organizations have been vital to their success. Finally, Robles said,

We need to learn from the students' experiences in our schools and to not repeat mistakes that we have made in the past. We need to continue to listen to our families. There is always something new to learn from them.

(2018, p. 11)

Achieving Goals

According to Maslow, when people have their basic survival, emotional, and social needs met, they are more prepared to set and realize their goals (Maslow, 1943/2000). In an interview in *Psychology Today*, Walsh, an expert on families overcoming trauma, says it is important to continue to work with the whole family (Pogosyan, 2017). As she puts it, "the whole is greater than the sum of its parts" (p. 2).

This is a time to work with families on their future goals. How can the school directly or through referrals support the family's goals, such as learning English, pursuing a GED, or going to classes? What goals does the family have for their children? Often maintaining family unity supersedes academic or financial goals, which may conflict with advice from counselors and teachers. For example, a family may prefer that a child goes to a nearby two-year college rather than leaving home to attend a major university even if they qualify for financial aid. Chapter 2 discusses ways to find out about their goals and priorities rather than predetermining what they should be.

According to Walsh, this is also a time for families to learn more about their communities beyond their immigrant groups (Pogosyan, 2017). Provide interpretation and encourage families to participate in school events involving other families. However, she emphasizes that this doesn't mean families should cut themselves off from their past. "If you were to cut off a plant from its roots and transplant it elsewhere, it will not survive. You have to bring some of its roots with it" (p. 2).

Involve immigrant families in decision-making and find out what enrichment activities the families might like, such as art, music, sports, or drama activities after-school, on weekends, or during summers. Families may meet other families through these events and expand their support networks (see Chapter 9 for ideas for partnerships, funding, and volunteers to support these activities).

Angry Families

All families, especially when they are under stress, may become angry about things that happen at school and affect their child negatively. The following scenario exemplifies how an administrator can deal with it calmly and show respect for the family's concerns.

Scenario: Failing Test Scores

Mrs. Chung, a Korean parent who had a son in third grade, came to the principal's office at the end of the year extremely angry because the third-grade teacher just told her that her son would be held back because he failed the state exam. Mr. Sandoval, the school's principal, put off a visit to a teacher's classroom so he could see her immediately. He also called in the library assistant, who spoke Korean and knew about confidentiality, to help with interpretation if needed. As the meeting progressed, he learned that Eric Chung, the third grader, had received all As and Bs throughout the year. Mrs. Chung was angry that her child was being held back based on the results of one test. If she had known he was having trouble, she would have gotten him extra help after school or on weekends, but now it was too late. Mr. Sandoval let Mrs. Chung finish explaining the situation in Korean as the library assistant interpreted. Mr. Sandoval said he understood Mrs. Chung's frustration. He then explained to Mrs. Chung that students who fail the test but do well in summer school are allowed to move on to the next grade. He asked if she would be willing to allow Eric to go to summer school. She agreed that this was a good alternative. Mr. Sandoval then accompanied Mrs. Chung to the school secretary's desk and asked him to help Mrs. Chung complete the necessary forms for Eric to go to summer school.

After Mrs. Chung left, Mr. Sandoval made a note to himself to discuss this type of situation (without names) with the teachers at their next meeting. How could a child get all As and Bs during the year and fail the state exam? Was the classroom work not aligned well enough with the exam? Was this the difference between teachers providing scaffolding during classroom work and their inability to help students during the exam? Should the school report the results of benchmark exams to families even if the results were not used as part of grades? Mr. Sandoval really did understand Mrs. Chung's frustration and hoped that with the teachers' assistance, he could prevent similar situations in the future.

Table 8.3 Dealing with Angry Families

• Deal with the problem as soon as possible.
• Know in advance what languages other than English your staff members speak and use them as interpreters when unexpected meetings arise, or use a phone interpreter if available quickly.
• Listen carefully and calmly to what the family member is saying without becoming defensive.
• Ensure that family members are treated as an equal and valued partner in their child's education.
• Refrain from using educational jargon.
• Work with the family member on a resolution to the problem.
• Do follow-up with the family member in a reasonable amount of time. Following up as promised helps build trust between the family and the school.
• Work with other stakeholders to prevent similar problems in the future.

No one relishes dealing with angry family members, but it is important to remain calm. In some cases, such as in the previous scenario, angry family members provide insights into problems that might not otherwise come to light and provide opportunities for improvement.

School resource officers and office staff, who may see the family first, should understand that family members may have made a concerted effort to come to the school to speak with school officials about their child's particular situation. They even may be missing pay to be at the school. Common tactics, such as asking the parent to return at another time or make an appointment, will often make matters worse. All staff should be reminded that all parents are to be treated courteously and professionally at all times and to direct difficult situations to the administration immediately. Every situation is an opportunity to build trust.

Activity: Community Resources

Purpose: The purpose of this activity is to locate community resources for families in need and create an up-to-date and local database.

Participants: People with knowledge of community resources and someone to establish and update the database for the district.

Preparation and resources: Contact personnel and agencies that may be able to provide lists of resources. Some states have directories already available that can serve as a starting point. For example, New Jersey has resource guides in English and Spanish with 27 different types of services ranging from food and housing to transportation and service dogs (New Jersey Department of Human Services, 2020). Local United Way databases also may provide information. There should be one person who is paid as part of their job to create and maintain this database. Perhaps, it could be the same person who is keeping the special needs database (see Chapter 7). The database should be readily available to educators, families, and staff who may need access quickly.

Description of activity: Make a list of needs of families living in poverty, such as food, housing, emergency shelter, transportation, legal services, and health care of all kinds, including dental care, mental health care, and immunizations. Match up those needs with organizations in the community that provide these services, including social service agencies, churches, medical clinics, shelters, and civic organizations.

For each entry on the database, there should be an outline of the services provided and the availability of languages other than English. There should be contact information, including addresses, phone numbers, and emails.

There also should be information about what identification or residency status is required to obtain assistance in order for families to decide if the resource is appropriate for them. Many families are afraid to access available assistance because they fear they will be detained or worse. Once the database is created, teachers and others could submit additions and updates to a central person who would enter them on the database. Since websites and organizations change frequently, it is important to keep the database up to date.

Options: Gather ideas from families for the database.

Activity: Questioning Prejudices

Purpose: The purpose of this activity is to help school district employees reflect on their own beliefs and practices. This activity was inspired by *Kwanzaa and Me* (Paley, 1996).

Participants: All employees of the school district.

Preparation and resources: Make the reflective questions available to staff members online or through hard copies. Give staff time to think about the questions. Be prepared to show the YouTube Video Prejudices (2019).

Description of Activity: Watch the three-minute YouTube Video Prejudices (2019). Give the staff time to think about the video and review the following questions. After the staff has had time to think about the questions, have small group discussion about what they could change in their own practices or believe the school or district should change and explain their reasoning. If time allows, share some of these ideas with the whole group and discuss next steps.

- **Reflective Questions:** When people see you for the first time, what assumptions do they make?
- Which of your characteristics do you wish people would recognize more?
- Can you think of times when you made a judgment about other people based on the way they looked or the group they belonged to?
- Have you ever avoided being with people based on the way they looked or the group they belonged to?
- What could you do to interact more with people who are different from you?
- How does this apply to nurturing relationships with families?

Options: Include families and/or students in these discussions.

Activity: Talking to Children about Diversity

Purpose: To facilitate families talking to their own children about diversity and individuality. Help children understand that being different is okay.

Participants: Families and teachers. Families should be grouped by grade or age level because the discussion families would have with their children would vary significantly between a 5-year-old and a 15-year-old. Make sure the program is made accessible through interpreters.

Preparation and resources: Prepare to project and read *I Am Enough* by Grace Byers (2018) or watch the YouTube video in which the book is presented by Storybook by Ms CeCe (2019). Arrange the room so families can be in small discussion groups. Have the text of the book translated into home languages with the page numbers labeled so families can follow along during the reading. Copies of the book or text also should be available in English during the discussion.

Description of activity: Place families in small discussion groups. Try to mix families from different backgrounds and provide interpreters as needed. Read the book or show the video. You can begin by asking families how they would use the book to teach their children about diversity, or you can begin by asking the group some questions about what the author means when she writes:

- ◆ "I am not meant to be like you: you are not meant to be like me" (p. 21)
- ◆ "And in the end, we are right here to live a life of love, not fear..." (p. 26)
- ◆ "I am enough" (p. 29)

Options: This activity could be done online with families at home. Other books, videos, or newspaper articles could be used as discussion starters. Families could be provided with children's books or a list of appropriate children's books to take home. Try to find books in the preferred languages of the family. A list of videos also could be provided. Other resources on this topic can be found at PBS, Common Sense Media, EmbraceRace, and the National Museum of African American History and Culture (see online support materials).

Relevant Literature

Efren Divided, by Ernesto Cisneros (2020), is a middle grades book that explores the life of a high school student whose world is turned upside down when his undocumented mother is deported back to Mexico. Efren is a U.S. citizen and has lived his whole life in the United States. As a young person, he has to grow up fast as he has to fill in as a caretaker for his younger siblings and help his father obtain funds to bring his mother back to the United States. This book illustrates the often precarious situations immigrant and refugee families have in the United States. Children and families will be reluctant to participate in school activities in case they expose their status to U.S. immigration authorities. *Chapter book.*

I Am Enough, by Grace Byers with pictures by Keturah A. Bobo (2018), shows multicultural children doing a variety of activities and not giving up. It emphasizes that our worth is not determined by how we look. When we try to be our best and treat others with kindness, "we are enough." *Picture book.*

The Other Side, by Juan Pablo Villalobos (2019), is a series of vignettes of Central American youth who made the journey to come to the United States as refugees. Each vignette describes some of the risks and challenges that these young people had to face. In addition to providing insight into these experiences, this book can give educators a better understanding of the family relationships that are part of the children's journey. Children may be coming to live with parents, but they may also be leaving parents to live with other relatives. The children themselves may have been traumatized by their journey. Also, as refugees, the children may be reluctant to share information about the family in case there is the risk of someone in the family being deported. *Chapter book.*

References

Adair, J. K. (2015, September). *The impact of discrimination on the early schooling experiences of children from immigrant families.* Migration Policy Institute. https://www.migrationpolicy.org/research/impact-discrimination-early-schooling-experiences-children-immigrant-families

Ann Frank House. (2019, September 19). *Prejudices explained.* [Video] YouTube. https://www.youtube.com/watch?v=IzEdSdvFLU0

Bureau of Labor Statistics. (2020, May 15). *Foreign-born workers: Labor force characteristics-2019.* U.S. Department of Labor. https://www.bls.gov/news.release/pdf/forbrn.pdf

Byers, G. & Bobo, K. A. (2018). *I am enough.* Balzer + Bray.

EdBuild. (n.d.). *Nonwhite school districts get $23 billion less than white districts despite serving the same number of students.* https://edbuild.org/content/23-billion

Gardner, L. (2019, December 16). *Community- and culturally-based approaches to trauma.* Immigrant Connections. https://www.immigrantsrefugeesand-schools.org/post/community-and-culturally-based-approaches-to-trauma

Gorski, P. (2019, April). Avoiding racial equity detours. *Educational Leadership,* 76(7), 56–61. http://www.edchange.org/publications/Avoiding-Racial-Equity-Detours-Gorski.pdf

Gross, H. (2020, April 22). *Perspective during COVID-19, teachers can support students using Maslow's hierarchy of needs.* https://www.ednc.org/perspective-during-covid-19-teachers-can-support-students-using-maslows-hierarchy-of-needs/

Maslow, A. H. (2000). A theory of human motivation. https://psychclassics.yorku.ca/Maslow/motivation.htm (Reprinted from 1943, *Psychological Review* 50, 370–396.)

Matisak, T. (Moderator). (2020, July 23). *How to talk to your kids about race.* [Webinar] PBS WHYY Virtual Commons series. https://www.youtube.com/watch?v=pRJ2tLyaYXs

National Center for Education Statistics. (2020a, May updated). *Characteristics of public school teachers.* https://nces.ed.gov/programs/coe/indicator_clr.asp

National Center for Education Statistics. (2020b, May updated). *Racial/ethnic enrollment in public schools.* https://nces.ed.gov/programs/coe/indicator_cge.asp

National Center for Homeless Education. (2019). *National overview.* http://profiles.nche.seiservices.com/ConsolidatedStateProfile.aspx

New Jersey Department of Human Services. (2020). *New Jersey resources 2020–2021.* https://nj.gov/humanservices/dds/documents/RD%202020-web.pdf

No Kid Hungry. (2020, April 30). *Emerging strategies and tactics for meal service during school closures related to the Coronavirus.* Center for Best Practices. http://bestpractices.nokidhungry.org/sites/default/files/2020-04/Strategies%20for%20Non-Congregate%20Meals%20During%20Coronavirus%20Closures_4-30.pdf

Ochieng, A. (2017, May 29). *Muslim schoolchildren bullied by fellow students and teachers.* National Public Radio (NPR). https://www.npr.org/sections/codeswitch/2017/03/29/515451746/muslim-schoolchildren-bullied-by-fellow-students-and-teachers

Paley, V. (1996). *Kwanzaa and me.* Harvard University Press.

Pogosyan, M. (2017, October 11). *What makes families resilient? Nurturing strength amid adversity.* https://www.psychologytoday.com/us/blog/between-cultures/201710/what-makes-families-resilient

Raikes, J. & Darling-Hammond, L. (2019, February 18). *Why our education funding systems are derailing the American dream.* Learning Policy Institute. https://learningpolicyinstitute.org/blog/why-our-education-funding-systems-are-derailing-american-dream

Robles, N. (2018). *Helping students heal through love and trust: A social worker's perspective on serving immigrant youth.* https://www.colorincolorado.org/article/helping-students-heal-through-love-and-trust-social-workers-perspective-serving-immigrant

Samuels, C. (2020). *The state of American education.* [Webinar] National Association of Secondary School Principals. https://www.nassp.org/event/state-of-american-education/

Scott, J., Moses, M. S., Finnigan, K. S., Trujillo, T., & Jackson, D. D. (2017). *Law and order in school and society: How discipline and policing policies harm students of color, and what we can do about it.* National Education Policy Center. http://nepc.colorado.edu/publication/law-and-order

Sheldon, S. B. & Jung, S. B. (2015, September). *The family engagement partnership student outcome evaluation.* Johns Hopkins University. http://www.pthvp.org/wp-content/uploads/2016/09/JHU-STUDY_FINAL-REPORT.pdf

Storybook by Ms CeCe. (2019, August 5). *I am enough,* read by Ms CeCe. [Video] YouTube. https://www.youtube.com/watch?v=mKKRQOs1AJ4

Urban Institute. (2019, March 14). Part *of us: A data-driven look at children of immigrants.* https://www.urban.org/features/part-us-data-driven-look-children-immigrants

Yoshikawa, H., Chaudry, A., Rendón García, S. A., Koball, H., & Francis, T. E. (2019, March). *Approaches to protect children's access to health and human services in an era of harsh immigration policy.* National Center for Children in Poverty. http://www.nccp.org/publications/pub_1222.html

9

Funding Family Engagement

Scenario: Reality Hits

Jada Miller had been an educator in Kansas for 20 years. In the last decade, she had seen a great influx of immigrant families especially from Latin America and Asia. Although the immigrant families seemed concerned about their children's education, they did not come to many traditional school activities, such as the open house, parent teacher association (PTA) meetings, or even Friday night football games. The students often lagged behind their native English-speaking peers in achievement test scores.

Miller, now a superintendent in a medium-sized district, had attended a professional conference where she heard a speaker talk about family engagement as a way to close the achievement gap among all students. The speaker even had ideas about different ways to engage immigrant families. She brought the speaker into her district to speak with principals and other administrators about a plan for engaging more of the families in the district.

After the presentation, Miller and the speaker left the room and asked the administrators to fill out a survey about the parts of the plan they liked and the challenges they might face in implementing the plan. Now, Miller was reading the comments. Almost all principals believed in the same things that the speaker was saying but one after another wrote that they didn't have the resources to implement anything new. They wrote things like, "My teachers are busy trying to improve test scores of the students and don't have time to deal with families too." "I don't have a budget to light, cool or heat the building for families at night or on weekends." "My teachers are already stressed out by the new reading curriculum. I really can't ask them to do anything more." Miller realized that she needed to address these very real concerns before trying to implement her plan.

Introduction

Much like administrators in the opening scenario, many educators feel pressure to stretch limited time and resources across many demands within the school community. Often strengthening the engagement of immigrant families is regarded as a low priority to be acted upon only if extra time and money are available.

This thinking is misguided as research is very clear about the benefits of family engagement. As discussed in Chapter 1, efforts to engage families yield many benefits to students, school organizations, and its families. Extensive research indicates that engaging families in children's education is one of the strongest predictors of children's development and educational achievement: school readiness, grades, test scores, and graduation (Weiss et al., 2018). The return on the time and resources devoted to strengthening parent and family involvement makes it one of the best investments a school can make.

Schools must be intentional in their search for the resources/support needed to enhance their family engagement work with immigrant families. Support comes in the form of volunteers, donations, partnerships, grants, federal funds, and fundraising. Such resources are best utilized when closely aligned with a school's family engagement goals.

A clear plan for family engagement with goals, activities, and possible resources designed to benefit immigrant families will help align goals and resources. Table 9.1 is a general example of a template linking a family engagement goal to possible resources. Steps needed to complete the template include:

1   Write a family engagement goal that is specific to needs of English learner (EL) and immigrant families. Best practice is to make SMART goals: specific, measurable, relevant, and timebound (Mind Tools Content Team, n.d.).
2   Identify activities to accomplish the goal.
3   Brainstorm and list possible funding sources that can support the activities. This column may be updated as additional resources become available.

Table 9.1 Sample Template for Family Engagement Plan

Campus Goal		
By the end of the fall semester, faculty and staff will have participated in 16 hours of development using the text, *Engaging the Families of ELs and Immigrants: Ideas, Resources and Activities*, to build their capacity to engage with immigrant families and identify one new practice for each grade level or department to implement with families in the Spring semester.		
Activities	**Resources Needed**	**Potential Funding Sources**
Faculty Book Study with *Engaging the Families of ELs and Immigrants: Ideas, Resources, and Activities*	Copies of the book Number of copies @ book price = total dollars needed.	Community Partnerships School-led fundraiser (Restaurant Spirit Night or Drive-a-Thon) Ask PTA/PTO for funds
Immigrant Family Panel from Chapter 1 activities	Printed questions Panelists Interpretation and translation costs as needed	Ask PTA/PTO or adopt-a-school partner to sponsor volunteer panelists, interpreters, and translation from a community organization that speak languages other than English, i.e., Refugee Resettlement Agency

Some states have formal requirements for district and family engagement plans related to state and national requirements. This campus plan may compliment such plans and is designed to intentionally target the engagement of immigrant families. Campuses are encouraged to adapt the template as needed.

Federal Monies under Every Student Succeeds Act

One major source of funding for engaging families in schools is the federal monies associated with the Every Student Succeeds Act (ESSA), Public Law 95-114 (Every Student Succeeds Act, 2015). The ESSA, passed in December 2015, reauthorized the Elementary and Secondary Act of 1965 and replaced the No Child Left Behind Act. Under ESSA, federal monies are awarded to school districts and campuses under different titles or sections of the law. Title 1, Part A Improving the Academic Achievement of the Disadvantaged and Title III Language Instruction for ELs and Immigrant Students are two key funding sources in the ESSA that may be utilized to support family engagement (United States Department of Education, n.d.-a).

A campus should work closely with their district's federal funding office or department to determine its eligibility to receive federal monies. It is important to know the amount of federal money to which the campus is entitled, how these funds flow from the district level to the campus, and allowable family engagement expenditures under the law's fiscal guidelines.

Title I Federal Funds

Title I monies provide financial assistance to districts and schools with high numbers or high percentages of children from low-income families to help ensure that all children meet challenging state academic standards. Under Title I, specific funding requirements exist for parental engagement.

School districts receiving more than $500,000 in Title I Part A funding are required to reserve at least 1 percent of its overall allotment to carry out family engagement activities (Shade, 2017; United States Department Education, n.d.-b). Ninety percent of this reserved funding must be distributed to schools and be used for at least one of the following activities:

◆ Supporting schools in training school staff regarding engagement strategies.
◆ Supporting programs that reach families at home, in the community and at school.
◆ Disseminating information on best practices focused on engagement, especially for increasing engagement of economically disadvantaged families.
◆ Giving subgrants to schools to collaborate with community-based organizations or businesses that have a track record of improving family engagement.
◆ Engaging in any other activities that the district believes are appropriate in increasing engagement (The Leadership Conference Education Fund, 2017).

Campuses should keep these required activities in mind as they plan their family engagement program. For example, funding a family literacy program would be an allowable expense for a campus qualifying for Title I monies. And in the case of campuses that serve the families of ELs and or immigrants, Title III funds are also available from the school district.

Title III Federal Funds

Title III provides federal monies to districts and schools for the education of ELs and those schools with a significant increase in immigrant students. Under ESSA, the purpose of Title III funds is to ensure that ELs and immigrant students attain English proficiency and meet academic achievement in English (National Clearinghouse for English Language Acquisition, n.d.). A requirement of Title III funds is to provide activities that promote EL family and community engagement. For example, a campus may choose to offer English as a Second Language classes to immigrant parents and families so that families may support their child(ren)'s academic achievement and become active participants in their education (United States Department of Education, 2016a).

Title II and IV Federal Funds

Although less common, ESSA also provides Title II Part A and IV Part A funding that may serve as additional monetary sources to support family engagement efforts. Title II Part A funds may be utilized to provide professional development to educators on family engagement practices (Dahlin, 2017; United States Department of Education, 2016b). Title IV Part A, Student Support and Academic Enhancement grants, may promote community and parent involvement in schools under section 4108 on Safe and Healthy Students (United States Department of Education, 2016c). Activities requesting funding through Title II and IV must meet allowable expenditures as authorized by the law.

Although Titles I–IV are all federal funds, schools may find these programs are operated under different offices at the district level. As a result, a campus may find it necessary to coordinate its family engagement plans with multiple persons or directors in the central office, unless there is a designated family engagement office through which funding requests may be made. It is recommended that school personnel familiarize themselves with their respective state documents related to federal Title funding. Such documents inform campuses as to the spending guidelines and or allowable expenditures for the funds.

Partnerships

Working with multiple organizations in the form of a specific partnership offers many advantages. The work and costs of family engagement can be spread across several organizations. Additionally, the participating organizations bring strengths and perspectives to promote the success of the program.

Organizations that Support Immigrants

Many faith-based organizations are actively involved in supporting immigrant and refugee families and may serve as an excellent link between schools and families. Such organizations also offer many specialized services to support refugees. Common services offered to refugees include cultural orientation to the community; interpretation and translation; links to health care;

educational access (i.e., adult English as Second Language (ESL) classes); and assistance with housing, food, and clothing. Refugee families also receive assistance in enrolling students in schools.

Schools may find it helpful to visit the U.S. Department of Health and Human Services' Office of Refugee Resettlement website (https://www.acf.hhs.gov/) to learn which agencies and organizations serve their state and or region. The site also provides information on each state's refugee coordinator as well as information on funding available to schools and/or refugee resettlement agencies from the U.S. Refugee School Impact Program. Approximately, $15,000,000 is available annually to 41 states to fund efforts to support refugees with family engagement, academic support, interpretation, mentoring support, and/or mental health services (Gardner, 2020).

Knowledge of such organizations and agencies can help schools identify resources to help support their family engagement efforts. For example, the Alliance for Multicultural Community Services (https://thealliancetx.org/) in Houston, Texas, offers numerous programs in addition to core refugee resettlement services. One program is the Alliance Language Network, which is able to offer interpretation and translation services in over 70 languages. The majority of its interpreters are former refugees who could also help the school gain cultural insight and understanding of the needs for its refugee and immigrant families. See Chapter 10 for more examples of community-based organizations that partner with schools.

Adult ESL Programs

Rural districts or communities that are new destinations for immigrant families may find Adult ESL Programs a valuable partner (Shiffman, 2019). Adult instructors in ESL programs are uniquely positioned to serve as a bridge between school districts and immigrant families. Instructors may share school district information, answer questions about U.S. schooling, and serve as facilitators at school-sponsored events. Districts should maintain regular communication with adult ESL programs and ensure they have access to updated district information and resources for immigrant families. Additionally, ESL instructors can offer insight to districts on the many challenges immigrant families face in supporting their child's education that may otherwise be overlooked.

Other Community Partnerships
Parent Teacher Associations/Organizations

PTAs and parent teacher organizations (PTOs) are helpful in creating partnerships with businesses, civic groups, and organizations to help the school engage immigrant families. National PTA has a free downloadable toolkit to assist PTAs in promoting a more diverse and inclusive membership (see on-line support materials). The toolkit suggests that PTAs create alliances with community groups, churches, and business organizations to establish networks of support beyond the school for all families, especially immigrants. Outside support networks can assist with the following: (a) Identify community members who may help translate materials or interpret at school events; (b) Find local churches operating youth-focused programs or ESL programs for parents; (c) Come across parents in local groups and organizations who may be interested in leadership opportunities; (d) Locate outside groups and organizations willing to sponsor or co-sponsor school events; (e) Discover alternative venues suitable for PTA and other school events; and (f) Invite leaders from community organizations to co-host PTA and or school activities in an effort to involve diverse community role models and foster alliance with external groups. Using PTAs or PTOs to help create support networks for families is a valuable resource that is available at no cost to the school and a critical link for immigrant families.

Service and Faith Based Organizations

Almost all faith-based organizations have service associations and there are civic clubs such as Lions or Elks. Learn about an organization before contacting it and see where its services might best fit your needs.

For example, Rotary Clubs are an excellent source of assistance for schools needing additional support in reaching out to culturally and linguistically diverse families. Clubs often choose to adopt a specific school and support it with volunteers and resources. Such an example is Wooldridge Elementary School in the Austin Independent School District in Austin, Texas. The school has been the West Austin Rotary Club's (https://portal.clubrunner.ca/7185/) community service project for more than 23 years. Rotary members are involved in reading to classes, assisting with family literacy and math nights, mentoring individual students, and providing financial support to the schools' outreach efforts.

In South Carolina, more than 1,500 churches have been recruited to adopt schools and assist them in helping meet students' basic needs. For example, churches become reading buddies by providing students with backpacks filled with nonperishable items and adding a book for children to read when not in schools (Vara-Orta, 2018).

Blessings in a Backpack

Blessings in a Backpack is a national organization that targets hunger and strives to feed children on the weekend through a backpack program (see online support materials). The program spans 45 states and Washington DC. Churches or service clubs may wish to come together to support such a project.

Recruiting Volunteers

With tight budgets, educators often feel they can barely fulfill their basic educational responsibilities, let alone provide services to the community. However, volunteers can help stretch the budget. The independent sector reports the average price per hour of volunteer time in the United States is a little over $27.00 (Independent Sector, 2020). One example of the value of volunteer hours comes from the Austin Partners in Education in Austin, Texas. In its 2020 report it noted $455, 197 of human capital value had been donated by volunteers for the Austin Independent School District. This figure was based on the calculation of 17,900 volunteer hours in schools @$25.43 per hour (Austin Partners in Education, n.d.).

Retired Volunteers

The good news is that with the aging population, many people are retiring with extensive skills and relatively good health. They no longer want to be tied down to a regular job, but they also don't want to stay home all day. Depending on their skills, they can help in the library or nurse's office, offer evening classes in English as a second language for immigrant families, or organize after-school or weekend arts, music, or other activities that use school facilities and work directly with family engagement events. They may also help with clerical work or the work of teaching assistants, allowing others to have a more flexible schedule.

Contact retirement villages and apartments for independent living and community programs for senior citizens. When one or two people have positive experiences at the school, they help to recruit more people they know.

High School Volunteers

High school students are a great source of volunteers. Many students belong to organizations or clubs which require them to earn community service hours, i.e., the National Honor Society. High schoolers come from the community and often speak the native languages of the families. Additionally, they may bring special skills that can be utilized at family events. For example, a school sponsoring a community health fair can use students enrolled in pre-nursing programs to help with taking blood pressure, do eyesight and hearing screenings, and hand out information to families. One high school

PTA organized a community Trunk or Treat event at Halloween for the families of its community. Over 30 high school organizations such as Drill Team, Girls' Basketball, Drama Club, Media Club, Latin Club, Band, and Choir decorated a trunk and provided games for families to play at the event. The students' energy and language skills helped all families feel welcome. High school sports teams in off season can help organize after-school soccer, softball, volleyball, tag football, or other teams at the elementary or middle schools. (Adults are needed to be available for emergencies.) Many immigrant families are interested in having low-cost or free after-school activities available for their children.

College and University Volunteers

College or technical school students are also an excellent resource for volunteers that can expand family engagement offerings. At some colleges or universities, there are civic engagement, outreach, or service-learning offices that help match community organizations looking for hands-on experiences in the community. If this type of office does not exist at the local college or university, public schools can contact college departments that offer classes in the subjects where help is needed. For example, college students studying a foreign language may be able to help with translation of school newsletters for families. Some universities, such as the University of Texas Rio Grande Valley, even offer classes in translation. Students studying educational leadership or administration may welcome practical experiences in assisting with family engagement nights or activities. College students also can offer a variety of workshops for families at your school, including tax preparation by accounting students, helping your child to read by education students, or art classes by art majors.

Nearby universities may also have multilingual students studying in the field of counseling, psychology, or social work, needing internship experiences. Such students may make an excellent source of additional support for emergent bilinguals and their families.

Volunteer Initiatives

Schools also may wish to consider running a volunteer pledge program through their campus' PTA. The National PTA Program (https://www.pta.org/) promotes a volunteer initiative titled *Three for Me* which encourages families/parents to dedicate three hours of their time at school, home, or the community during the school year. PTO Today (https://www.ptotoday.com/) has a similar volunteer kit known as *2 Hour Power* that can also be downloaded for free.

Grant Writing

Securing a grant is another way to support family engagement programming. Schools may consider putting together a team of stakeholders who are willing to look for grants. Stakeholders may include teachers, families, and community members. This team can work to identify funding needs of the campus' family engagement program and seek out available grants.

Online Grant Search Tools

A district's central office may help schools find potential grants and prospective donors. Such grant offices may subscribe to online databases and search tools that allow a campus to look for potential funding sources. Campus grant writing teams should inquire about these tools and may ask the district to invest in subscriptions. Some examples of online search tools include Candid and Grant Station (see online support materials).

Campuses may also wish to utilize free grant search tools such as grants4teachers to look for grants (see online support materials). The site is continuously updated and offers an option for schools to sign up to receive a free weekly email newsletter containing grant alerts.

National PTA Grants

National PTA has partnered with companies such as Bayer and Mathnasium to award grants to schools to host family festivals in Science, Math, Inventions, Tech, and Game Nights. Schools may visit the National PTA site to sign up for alerts and updates on grant opportunities related to family engagement activities.

Numerous free resources, including a how-to toolkit for family festivals, are available at the site (see online support materials). Templates for soliciting donations to help fund family festivals are found in the online toolkit as well as promotional materials in English and Spanish. Additionally, the site contains examples of science experiments that can be done at home with videos and written guides. These are especially useful for immigrant families who may be reluctant to attend a school festival but wish to support learning in the home. Since only a few PTA grants are awarded yearly, the information on the website makes it relatively easy for a school to host family festivals even without a grant.

Gardening Grants

Gardening has been identified as a valuable activity for ELs and immigrant families as it helps create community across cultures (Raby, 2016). Therefore, schools wishing to involve immigrant families in the school may be interested in creating school gardens with the help of a grant. The KidsGardening.org website offers grants, grant writing tips, and webinars to schools wishing to promote this idea. The website also maintains an extensive list of other gardening grants.

Fundraising Events

Although parents, administrators, and teachers dread fundraising, most schools find it necessary. Schools may wish to look for fundraising activities that are fun and build community with families. Such activities include hosting restaurant spirit nights and drive-a-thons. Schools may also look to online fundraising especially when social gatherings may be limited as is the case during the COVID-19 pandemic.

Restaurant Spirit Nights

Another way to raise funds and build community is to host a restaurant spirit night (Bizzarri, 2020). Many national restaurant chains have information on their websites regarding spirit nights. The school and participating restaurant invite the school community to dine at the restaurant on a set afternoon or evening. The restaurant then donates back an agreed upon percentage of its sales from the spirit night to the school. Schools may wish to link restaurant spirit nights to a specific event like Back to School. Schools can plan a School Kickoff night that builds excitement for the start of school. Volunteers can agree to pass out name tags to families and take group photos if desired.

Drive-a-Thons

Schools and community organizations can raise funds by test driving cars. Most of the major car companies have programs in which they give back to schools when they get people in for test drives. Schools may wish to consider holding their event in conjunction with another event such as a bake sale or car wash. When planning an event, also consider having music, food, and beverages as a way to encourage attendees, which may include families, to linger or be entertained while waiting to test drive. Schools or organizations will need to have multiple volunteers on hand for the event.

Drive-a-Thons are highly popular, and car dealers are often limited to the number of events sponsored per year. Schools should reach out to dealerships early in the school year to secure the event.

Crowdfunding

Online fundraising, crowdfunding, is becoming an increasingly popular fundraising method for teachers and schools. Special projects can be funded by raising small amounts of money via the internet from a large number of people. Donors may include businesses, organizations, friends, families, and school alumni wishing to provide support.

Popular crowdfunding sites like Donors Choose, Digital Wish, and Fundly help connect schools/teachers with donors who desire to help fund classroom or school projects (see online support materials). Schools select a crowdfunding platform on which to tell their story, upload photos, and accept donations. Schools, teachers, and parent–teacher groups may wish to investigate the various platforms available to determine which is most appropriate. Not all platforms are free. Tips for successful crowdfunding include the following:

◆ Pick your platform.
◆ Set up your campaign and be specific about what the donations are going toward.
◆ Use visuals, pictures, and videos, in addition to text.
◆ Make use of social media to spread the word, i.e., Facebook, Instagram, and Twitter.
◆ Track your crowdfunding campaign's progress and regularly update progress toward your goal for donors to see.
◆ Look at other crowdfunding campaigns for successful ideas.

Conclusion

Schools wishing to strengthen their engagement programs for immigrant families will find additional resources within their community and districts to support these efforts. Intentional efforts to seek out these resources must be ongoing. Schools must be prepared to clearly articulate the support and resources needed by the campus to partner with all its families. This can be accomplished by developing a family engagement plan with program goals, activities, resources needed, and possible funding sources. An ongoing wish list of suggested monetary or material donations to support family engagement that aligns with goals should be maintained.

Schools should keep careful track of volunteer hours, donations of goods, services, and money for future grant applications that may ask for such information and or community partners who may ask for past examples of support given for family engagement. Campuses may also wish to regularly take pictures of activities and gather family comments to document their success in engaging all its school families so that they may be shared on social media and included in thank yous to organizations supporting the school. Schools must be ready to respond when resources are offered, and grant opportunities become available.

Activity: Family Engagement Funding Team

Purpose: The purpose of this activity is to establish a team to look for available resources to strengthen family engagement efforts.

Participants: A group of six to eight stakeholders representing a cross section of stakeholders—teachers, family, and community members.

Preparation and resources: A school administrator or teacher leader will organize a start-up meeting by sending invitations and developing an agenda. Print copies of the agenda and any needed handouts such as the school's family engagement plan.

Description of activity: Host a kickoff meeting of school stakeholders who may be interested in serving on a family engagement funding team for the school. Team members review the list of potential funding opportunities presented in Chapter 9 and link to the campus' family engagement plan. District personnel could be invited as guests to discuss central office support for grant writing and campus eligibility for Title I–IV federal funds.

Option: Another option would be to have school faculty as a whole read Chapter 9 and brainstorm together which funding source would be a good fit for the campus and its family engagement efforts and identify volunteers from the school who would be willing to seek funding and donations from community groups.

Activity: Making Connections

Purpose: The purpose of this activity is to find potential new partners and sources of volunteers. This activity may be especially useful in locating community members who speak languages in addition to English that can help the school meet the language needs of school families.

Participants: Anyone interested in the school community.

Preparation and resources: Prepare a volunteer recruitment flyer that can be distributed in the community to identify persons who would be willing to volunteer in the school. The flyer should include suggestions about volunteer recruitment opportunities at the school. Included in the list should be an opportunity for community members who speak a language other than English to help at the school.

Description of activity: Ask school staff and others interested in the school and their families what community organizations they participate in. This could include religious organizations, service organizations, gardening or art societies, museums, college organizations, or others. Then, ask the participant if they would take a flyer to a meeting or a leader in the organization or share via social media. The flyer would ask members if they would like to partner with the school, provide contact information and possible partnership contributions. A major need is to identify volunteers who speak a language other than English. Additional volunteer activities may include cleaning the campus on weekends, collecting school supplies for needy students, or sponsoring special events on campus. Have someone gather these flyers and contact organizations that are interested in forming partnerships and make arrangements for the partnership. Although this will initially take some time, it will repay the effort in the long run.

Options: Ask staff members and families what businesses and churches they have contacts with. Send out a similar flyer but include options for Adopting a School or contributing for specific projects, materials, or equipment. For example, some businesses or churches may be willing to donate older computers or printers that could be checked out by students and families.

Relevant Literature

Sitti's Secret, by Naomi Shihab Nye (1994), is a book that describes the life of a girl of Palestinian descent who lives in the United States with her family. The book describes her visit to her grandmother living in Palestine. She is unable to speak to her grandmother, so her father translates for her. Although they cannot communicate verbally, they spend time together sharing her grandmothers' activities like baking flatbread and making lemonade using the lemons from her grandmother's tree. The emphasis of the story is that although people do different things and eat different foods, they have much in common. *Picture book.*

They Call Me Guëro: A Border Kid's Poems, by David Boles (2018), is narrated by a Mexican American boy, nicknamed Guëro, who lives on the border between the United States and Mexico. The book captures the importance of family traditions and celebrations as well touching on immigration issues on the border as it is set in 2018. *Poetry book.*

References

Austin Partners in Education. (n.d.). *APIE's impact.* https://www.austinpartners.org/

Bizzarri, A. (2020, July 6). 37 restaurants that do school fundraisers. *We Are Teachers.* https://www.weareteachers.com/restaurants-that-do-school-fundraisers/

Dahlin, M. (2017, May 9). All in the family: Supporting students through family engagement in ESAA. *New America.* https://www.newamerica.org/education-policy/edcentral/all-family-supporting-students-through-family-engagement-essa

Every Student Succeeds Act, 20 U.S.C. § 6301. (2015). https://www.congress.gov/114/plaws/publ95/PLAW-114publ95.pdf

Gardner, L. (2020, November 12). *The U.S. Refugee School Impact program.* [Video] YouTube. https://www.youtube.com/watch?t=3601&v=eM4h10HLMSk&feature=youtu.be

Independent Sector. (2020, July). *Value of volunteer time.* https://independentsector.org/value-of-volunteer-time-2020/

Mindtools Content Team. (n.d.). *Smart goals: How to make your goals achievable.* https://www.mindtools.com/pages/article/smart-goals.htm

National Clearinghouse for English Language Acquisition. (n.d.). *Title III grant FAQs.* https://ncela.ed.gov/title-iii-grant-faqs#:~:text=Title%20III%20is%20a%20part,and%20meet%20state%20academic%20standards

Raby, A. (2016, February 26). Why gardening education is perfect for English language learners. *Food Corps.* https://foodcorps.org/why-gardening-education-is-perfect-for-english-language-learners/

Shade, C. (2017, February 21). ESSA parent and family engagement. *Ready Rosie.* https://www.readyrosie.com/essa-parent-and-family-engagement/

Shiffman, C. D. (2019). Supporting immigrant families and rural schools: The boundary spanning possibilities of an adult ESL program. *Education Administration Quarterly*, 55(4), 537–570. https://doi.org/10.1177/0013161X18809344

The Leadership Conference Education Fund. (2017, September). *Every Student Succeeds Act: A guide for advocates.* http://civilrightsdocs.info/pdf/education/ESSA/ESSA-Guide.pdf

United States Department of Education. (n.d.-a). *ESSA table of contents.* https://www2.ed.gov/policy/elsec/leg/essa/legislation/index.html

United States Department of Education. (n.d.-b). *Improving basic programs operated by local education agencies Title I Part A.* https://www2.ed.gov/programs/titleiparta/index.html#:~:text=Title%20I%2C%20Part%20A%20(Title, ensure%20that%20all%20children%20meet

United States Department of Education. (2016a). *Non-regulatory guidance: English Learners and Title III of the Elementary and Secondary Education Act*. https://www2.ed.gov/policy/elsec/leg/essa/essatitleiiiguidenglishlea rners92016.pdf

United States Department of Education. (2016b). *Non-regulatory guidance for Title II Part A: Building systems of support for excellent teaching and learning*. https://www2.ed.gov/policy/elsec/leg/essa/essatitleiipartaguidance. pdf

United States Department of Education. (2016c). *Non-regulatory guidance: Student support and academic enrichment grants*. https://www2.ed.gov/ policy/elsec/leg/essa/essassaegrantguid10212016.pdf

Vara-Orta, F. (2018, September 25). New money and energy to help schools connect with families. *Education Week*. https://www.edweek.org/ew/ articles/2018/09/26/new-money-and-energy-to-help-schools.html

Weiss, H. M., Lopez, E., Caspe, M. (2018). *Carnegie challenge paper: Joining together to create a bold vision for next generation family engagement*. Global Family Research Project. https://globalfrp.org/content/download/419/ 3823/file/GFRP_Family%20Engagement%20Carnegie%20Report.pdf

10

Success Stories

Introduction

Schools across the country face a similar challenge in trying to strengthen partnerships with immigrant families given rapidly changing student demographics. They are grappling with what it takes to successfully work with families of immigrants and emergent bilinguals in their communities. This chapter presents examples from a variety of school districts, family leadership initiatives, and community-based organizations that have had a high level of success in strengthening engagement with immigrant families. Innovative ideas, practices, and principles are presented to illustrate how this important work can be accomplished in different contexts.

School Success Stories

Districts vary in their success with this undertaking. This section highlights four districts from across the country that may serve as models for engaging immigrant families and offer lessons learned from the work. Their successes evolved over time and centered on the desire to embrace families as essential partners in student learning.

Klein Independent School District (ISD)
While other districts struggle to engage immigrant families, Klein ISD, in suburban Houston, has succeeded by making family engagement a pillar of

their mission. From Superintendent Dr. Jenny Mc Gowan to the staff at its 49 schools, family engagement is a high priority. This is reflected in the district's strategic plan which lists building community as one of its three goals. (see Figure 10.1). The goal of building community is accomplished through: (a) relationships, mentoring, and partnerships; (b) engaging, educating, and equipping families; and (c) being culturally responsive.

According to Family Engagement Director Maria Ovalle Lopez (personal communication, October 2, 2020), one of the defining moments was when the district made a commitment to send a group of 14 educators and community members to Harvard's Family Engagement Institute to learn about the Dual Capacity Building Framework (DCBF) for Family School Partnerships (see Figure 10.2). The Framework supports building the skills and confidence of families to partner with schools and advocate for their children. At the same time, educators learn to respect the expertise of families and overcome assumptions about families, especially those who are emergent bilinguals. Each summer, except during the pandemic, the school district has sent a group of educators and family members to the Harvard training.

The district also created organizational conditions that build family engagement by placing the program under College and Career Pathways to support the district's mission of exiting with a purpose—college and career ready.

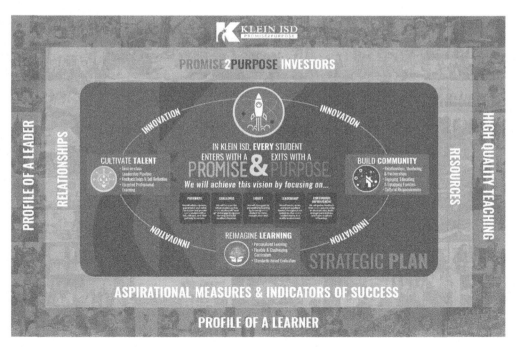

Figure 10.1 Klein Independent School District Strategic Plan.

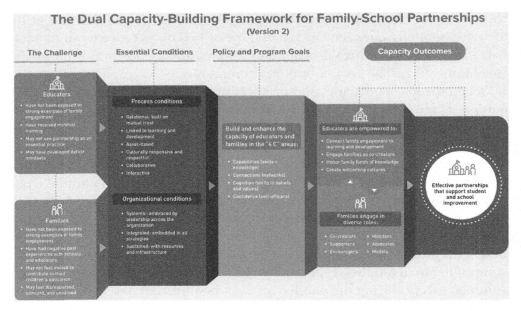

Figure 10.2 Dual Capacity Building Framework (Mapp and Bergman, 2019).

Ms. Ovalle Lopez notes that Klein's family engagement programs are intentionally designed to celebrate families' cultures, provide opportunities for respectful communication, and to create a sense of community for all families at every campus. All Title I schools have a family liaison to welcome and assist families as needed. Eleven elementary campuses plus one high school campus offer classes through their Parent University. Course offerings are designed based on families' interests and to help families link student learning to post-secondary readiness. Courses are offered in English, Spanish, and Vietnamese.

When planning family classes, Ms. Ovalle Lopez emphasized that schools should not make assumptions about what they think families need. "Best intentions don't serve parents … find out what they want." Also, rather than having each school reinvent the wheel and create their own parent engagement activities each year, the school district encourages campuses to share their ideas with one another through the use of a repository.

As a model Texas Education Agency school for parent engagement, school leaders are frequently asked what they would recommend to other schools. Klein suggests three key items: (a) work to build the capacity of staff to engage families, (b) empower parents to lift up the community-parents so they can help drive family engagement, and (c) have an "ear" in the community that hears from families and can speak to families. One story illustrated the key points. A Spanish-speaking mother, who attended parent literacy training offered by the district, returned to her family's apartment complex and started a book club with other immigrant families to encourage neighborhood children to read more. She is an example of how empowered families can help promote learning outside the classroom.

Rogers Public Schools, Arkansas

As U.S. schools become increasingly diverse, some districts may find themselves facing rapidly changing student demographics. Rogers Public Schools is an example. Currently, the district has an enrollment of approximately 16,000 students and has seen its Latinx population grow from 3 percent to almost 50 percent over the last 20 years. Additionally, it also serves an increasing number of Marshallese students.

From the beginning, Rogers Public Schools saw the need to create trusting relationships between families and the district and make sure that immigrant families felt welcome. The school board set the tone by adopting the mission that Rogers schools would provide "an environment of educational excellence where all belong, all learn, and all succeed." To help make that a reality, they approved creating a student relations liaison position that would specifically support students and families from diverse backgrounds.

Carlos Amargós, outreach specialist, shared the district's philosophy: "This [school] is our business and we're here to serve our customers [all families]" (personal communication, November 30, 2020). The district values communication with families and seeks input from them. Multiple communication approaches include Spanish radio, district YouTube channel in Spanish and Marshallese, and social media such as Facebook and WhatsApp. Bilingual flyers are also placed in restaurants and stores around the community about educational events. Mr. Amargós emphasized the importance of teaching immigrant families the various ways to communicate with the district.

Learning to bridge cultures was an important part of Rogers' success. Professional Development was needed to help the district's teachers and administrators dispel myths and misinformation held about immigrant families. For example, one misconception held was that Latinx students only came from Mexico rather than a variety of Spanish-speaking countries. At the same time, efforts were made to help families learn how the school system worked in Rogers. This effort began at the high school level as a result of a request from student leaders.

The Hispanic Ambassadors, a Latinx student leadership group, was formed by the administration to seek advice on how to integrate the students' culture into the high school. Traditional activities such as student pep rallies, dances, and some sports held little relevance for the students. Students asked administration to engage their families in their schooling. As a result, the parent group, PADRES (Parents Advancing Readiness in Educational Studies), was started with the goal of providing Spanish-speaking parents the opportunity to come together to gain the skills and knowledge needed to help support their child(ren)'s educational aspirations such as the pathway to college admission.

PADRES has since evolved to meet the needs of families on individual campuses. At Rogers New Technology High School, PADRES meets approximately once a month or about seven or eight times per year. Topics emerge based on family needs and what is taking place during the school year. For example, fall workshops are organized around college planning and FAFSA (Free Application for Federal Student Aid). Spring topics may include college entrance, summer internship opportunities, and/or the selection of courses for the following school year. Topics offered also include how-to skills such as setting up an email account and checking student attendance and grades. Dr. Arbuckle shared, "People participate because of the trust, they continue… return each month because we are providing them with information, they may not have access to otherwise" (personal communication, September 30, 2020).

Rogers has learned how to successfully reach out to its immigrant families and welcome them into the school community. The district listens to families' needs and wants and views families as important partners for student success.

Shelby County Schools

Despite a busy schedule, educators and administrators in Shelby County Schools in Memphis, Tennessee, realized that implementing a strong family engagement program for immigrant families was worth the time and could create effective advocates for the schools. Yesenia Ubaldo, Department of Family and Community Engagement advisor, said at first, she had to work hard at pitching a new program to schools, but after a few years with Conectando Familias or Families Connect in the district, principals are asking that the program be expanded to their schools (personal communication, October 28, 2020).

For Ubaldo, the keys to success have been a passion for partnering with immigrant families and collaboration both inside and outside the school district. The program grew out of the Padres Comprometidos *Unidos* curriculum, which was being offered by Latino Memphis at their offices. Ubaldo liked the program, which helps immigrant parents understand the U.S. school system and includes parents talking to the principal at their child's school about issues important to them. However, to serve the families of the 10,000 emergent bilinguals in Shelby County Schools, she believed the program needed to be moved into the schools.

One of the reasons immigrant families often are missing from family engagement programs is the lack of opportunities offered in their native language. For this reason, Ubaldo began by presenting the *Unidos* curriculum to the English as a Second Language Department leads, Andrew Duck and Debra Frantz, with the vision of having the Bilingual Cultural Mentors implement the program at the school level in their native language. This led to the partnership between Christina A. Villalpando, Bilingual Cultural Counselor with the ESL department, and Ubaldo. Next, they worked with Jose Rodriguez at the headquarters of Padres Comprometidos in San Antonio to obtain a grant and do the original training in the Shelby County Schools with a family specialist and bilingual mentors from six schools and two to three parents from each of those schools. The district now does its own training with updates from Padres Comprometidos and attendance at an annual conference. Although most of the training is done in Spanish, the training also has been implemented in Arabic and English. Shelby schools have made other modifications too such as adding a component about accessing district and student information online.

The program now has many more partners, including faith-based organizations, who provide childcare during in-person sessions; the library, which helps families get library cards; and local community colleges who explain entrance requirements and financial aid. An unexpected benefit of the program has been that some family members have entered college themselves.

In advising other school districts, Ubaldo says, "Gather as many supporters as you can to help you succeed." She adds that you need to know the resources in the schools and the community and then "knock on doors." After participating in the program, the families also become supporters and encourage other immigrant families to become involved with the schools.

Success requires more than money; it requires a passion for engaging disengaged families and for what families mean to the schools according to Ubaldo and Villalpando. Ubaldo adds, "You need to love what you are doing, and you will see results."

Washoe County Schools

Washoe County Schools in Reno, Nevada, engages families by listening more than telling. This is a challenging task in a district that serves over 64,000 students, the majority of whom are students of color, 56.5 percent. The district's largest ethnic group is Hispanic, but family demographics also include immigrants from Afghanistan, Syria, and the Congo. Additionally, the district serves Native American families.

D' Lisa Crain, administrator for the family schools partnership program, leads the district's strategic work to place families as vital partners in support of their children's learning. This work has evolved over time to include various initiatives that are research based, sustainable, and stem from student and family needs. Initiatives are carefully selected and usually delivered at the school site by faculty who have a strong relationship with families and the community.

The district anchors its family engagement work with the Dual Capacity Building Framework (Figure 10.2). Crain explained:

> We kind of live by the federal Dual Capacity Building Framework for family school partnerships– so we really stay focused on how we help parents support learning outside the classroom … As well as how do we build the capacity of teachers to successfully partner with families and particularly families that don't look like or reflect the background of our teaching staff (personal communication, October 29, 2020).

One example of how the district builds teachers' capacity is by intentionally embedding family engagement into the professional learning offered to its educators. Recently, a grant funded 64 elementary literacy specialists to assist with the implementation of a new law on mandatory reading by third grade. As specialists met monthly for professional learning, family engagement was on the agenda alongside topics such as assessment, curriculum and instruction, and English learner (EL) development. Specialists learned how to engage families in support of the reading goal and to do so in a manner that honored families' knowledge.

Currently, the district offers *Blue Friday* every few months for its teacher leaders who are on special assignments in the district such as instructional coaches or teachers embedded in departments like English language development or special education. Blue Fridays are large conferences that offer sessions on various topics essential to these teacher leaders' work. Family engagement has been included as a session to allow for in-depth training on the dual-capacity framework and to explore what it looks like in practice on a campus.

Washoe County Schools have numerous examples of best practice initiatives such as the Parent Teacher Home Visit (n.d.) and parent graduation advocates who make use of the Early Warning Index (Allensworth, 2013). The initiatives are well-supported by the district, built over time, and evaluated for effectiveness in supporting student success.

Crain offered advice for schools wishing to strengthen engagement with immigrant families. It includes: (a) "listen first, don't lead with your own ideas … lead with the voices and needs of families," (b) lead with relationships and focus upon equity and antiracism, (c) provide space for teachers to reflect on the biases held about families' capacity to help support student learning, and (d) "connect the dots to data." Collect and use data to inform your program and to identify which populations are not being served.

Family Leadership Initiative Success Stories

Parent leadership initiatives are forming across the country (Henderson et al., 2016). Although the details and funding of each program differ, they share certain components. The community-based organizations focus on developing the abilities of families, including immigrants, to advocate for their children's education. In most cases, their staff reflects the communities they serve, and they develop the trust of immigrant groups.

Schools that are having difficulty reaching these communities can partner with one of the local initiatives or affiliates to build a bridge to immigrant families. Four different parent leadership initiatives are highlighted here; all share a desire to make the voices of immigrants heard and participate in educational decision-making that is important to their community.

Padres Comprometidos

Padres Comprometidos and its affiliates are bridges between schools and those families who are generally not engaged with the schools. The affiliates are mostly community-based organizations that serve the Hispanic population across the country. The organizations are part of the Hispanic community, understand the needs of that community, and have built trust with the families. When these organizations work closely with schools, everyone benefits according to Director Jose Rodriguez.

An essential part of the program is training about 2,000 parents a year on how to better participate in their children's education, using a trainer of trainers' model. Although most programs are completed in Spanish or English, some affiliates have translated the curriculum into Portuguese, Arabic, and Swahili.

The program, which is part of UnidosUS, helps recent immigrants better understand the U.S. school system, such as what is expected at a parent–teacher conference or what standardized test questions look like. At the middle school and high school levels, they help families support their children in preparing and applying for college and financial aid.

The parent curriculum was written by educators and is updated annually. The final activity is preparing family members to speak with the principal at a school one of their children attends. Rodriguez (personal communication, October 6, 2020) emphasizes that this is not a "gotcha" activity but one that helps principals understand that Hispanic families can be allies in engaging more families and raising student achievement. The program provides families with the confidence to advocate for their children's education. A group of families in New York even spoke with Mayor DiBlassio to ensure that schools were safe from U.S. Immigration and Customs Enforcement (ICE) raids as required by law.

Rodriguez says the community-based organizations can help educators remove some of the barriers that prevent many families from participating with the schools. For example, they can help schools find interpreters. Rodriguez has even successfully reached out to military language institutes for help with interpretation and translation. Transportation and work schedules also can be barriers. Rodriguez said that one affiliate in Los Angeles arranged to provide family training for custodians at midnight in the high-rise buildings where they worked. In Tampa, Florida, an affiliate had difficulty getting families to their offices in the downtown area, but when they collaborated with the local school system, they went from training 10 families to training 700.

When asked what schools could do better to reach Hispanic families, he said that schools need to honor the culture, language, and values of the families. Schools also need to have high expectations for all students. Rodriguez remembers as a teacher of emergent bilingual students, he was told the sessions on the Free Application for Federal Student Aid (FAFSA) were not open to his students because they were not going to college. Rodriguez responded, "Your job is to prepare every child to go to college."

Rodriguez also said that most Hispanics hold teachers in very high esteem and are unlikely to question them or to share problems because they see this as a breach of trust. They are trusting teachers with their most valuable possession, their child.

Parent Institute for Quality Education

Immigrant families need to understand the U.S. school system to increase academic achievement and support their children's path to college, and educators need to better understand the strengths and needs of families. The Parent Institute for Quality Education (PIQE) is one of the few community-based organizations that builds capacity among both families and educators.

Patricia Mayer, who has been with PIQE since its inception, says families and educators were living "in the same world, but different universes" (personal communication, October 9, 2020). Immigrant families often felt the schools did not recognize their knowledge of their own children. Educators sometimes felt immigrant families were not interested in their children's education because they didn't participate in expected ways. Through workshops,

PIQE works to break down these misunderstandings. The training for teachers, counselors, and administrators uses case studies to expose assumptions, biases, and barriers to family engagement.

At the end of the school workshops, participants work together to create a family engagement action plan, which is tailored to the local needs. Although the plans vary, educators are encouraged to create plans that "lift up the voices of families" and see the assets of all families. Administrators who make budget decisions need to be a part of the plan development to ensure the plan can be implemented.

Another accomplishment of PIQE is bringing together families from a variety of cultural, religious, and language backgrounds. Many of these families did not interact previously in the community yet come together in PIQE classes to work toward the success of all their children.

PIQE President and CEO Gloria Coral (personal communication, October 9, 2020) said the families have a shared sense of resiliency. She told the story of an Iraqi woman who had spent months with her children in a refugee camp without sufficient food, water, or shelter. During her PIQE parent engagement graduation ceremony, the woman shared the story of how much she and her children had overcome to be there but how the program had given her hope for her children's future. The testimonial was translated from Arabic to English and then English to Spanish. When it was spoken in Spanish, there was suddenly loud clapping from women who came from Mexico and Guatemala who understood her struggles and her dreams for the future.

The families also garnered government support for the program. The mayor of San Jose, California, was teary-eyed when an immigrant father shared his story at a parent engagement graduation ceremony. The father, who had just come from working in the fields, said "I am the architect of my son's future. He can take the bus to the fields or the bus to the university. I choose the university."

Although PIQE is headquartered in California, they work with schools in 13 states to help them reach about 18,000 families a year with curriculum in 16 languages. Mayer's first piece of advice to these schools is "don't waste the families' time." Families want to participate in activities that will directly benefit their children. If families feel they are valued and they can improve their children's education at school and at home, they will become more involved and bring other families with them.

She also shared her own experience as a teacher and said that having families involved is in the teacher's self-interest. As a bilingual teacher with 35 students and no aide, she had parents help in the classroom every day. There were so many interested parents that each only volunteered once every two weeks. "I couldn't have survived without parent help," Mayer said. She said it made her a better teacher and the parents became "super aware" of what it takes for a child to learn. She reminded us that when teachers want to improve students' education, "There is no greater force than the love of a mother for her child."

Portland Empowered

Most parent engagement communication involves schools providing information they think is important to families. Portland Empowered has turned that idea on its head.

The family leadership initiative in Portland, Maine, has created Shared Space Cafes to facilitate true dialogue between educators and families, especially immigrants. Rather than schools deciding what is important to share, families choose the topics and lead the discussions in their native languages. Families, staff, speakers of languages other than English, and English speakers are intentionally mixed at tables for small group discussions. An interpreter at each table translates from the native language to English rather than the other way around. For many educators, this is the first time they have been in a setting where English is not the dominant language. It gives them an idea of how immigrants feel during English-dominant conversations. The discussions during the Shared Space Cafes "blow out of the water" the myth that many schools have about parents not wanting to be involved in their children's education, according to staff member Pious Ali (personal communication, October 13, 2020).

In addition to the Shared Space Cafes, Portland Empowered has a Parent Engagement Partners (PEPs) program that is dedicated to amplifying the voices of those who are usually left out of educational decision-making. A parallel group is Youth Engagement Partners (YEPS), which helps high school students develop leadership skills and advocate for equity.

Families in Portland Empowered wrote a Parent and Family Engagement Manifesto that provides a framework for all family engagement in the district. The Manifesto emphasizes the importance of personal contact rather than robocalls or mass emails. Another principle in the Manifesto is creating safe spaces where everyone's expertise is valued. The Manifesto recommends schools track who is involved in decision-making and make accommodations, such as interpretation for families who are not normally included. The Manifesto also emphasizes the need to devote resources, including time and money, for family engagement to be successful.

Portland Empowered is part of the Youth and Community Engagement team at the Cutler Institute, which is housed at the University of Southern Maine. Portland Empowered works closely with schools and communities across the country. Ali, who has served on the Portland School Board himself, says that by establishing meaningful relationships with community partners, schools can reach out to immigrant families who already trust those partners and do much more than would otherwise be possible. These relationships are built on a shared interest in the well-being of the students and families.

OneAmerica

OneAmerica is one of a growing number of immigrant and refugee community-based organizations that work on projects that school districts can't do. As a power organization, they compare themselves to a labor union for immigrant and refugee causes, many of which concern children's education. A grass-roots organization, representing large numbers of immigrants from varying backgrounds in Washington State, they support candidates and lobby the state legislature for change.

Some of their greatest accomplishments are related to promoting bilingualism as an asset. For example, they pushed through a bill establishing a Seal of Biliteracy on transcripts and diplomas for students who can pass fluency tests in speaking, reading, and writing in English and another world language. They have increased dual language immersion programs in which native English speakers and native speakers of another language learn core curriculum together in both languages, usually beginning in kindergarten.

OneAmerica, which began after 9/11 in 2001, believes that the people closest to an issue or problem are the best ones to work for a solution. Their theory of change involves community organizing and leadership development in immigrant and refugee communities. They collaborate with other community-based organizations, such as The Road Map Project, which works to increase opportunities for students of color. They also collaborate with indigenous groups, who are working to revitalize native languages.

When asked how school districts nationwide could better engage emergent bilingual and immigrant families, OneAmerica Deputy Director Roxana Norouzi (personal communication, October 6, 2020) said that attitudes must change to embrace bilingualism as an asset rather than a deficit. She points to research that shows cognitive, identity, career, and cross-cultural understanding benefits from bilingualism.

OneAmerica supports a "Grow Your Own" approach to changing the composition of school labor forces, including interpreters. Norouzi says it doesn't make sense to go to Spain to recruit Spanish-speaking teachers. OneAmerica is confronting this issue on many fronts, including expanding teacher education programs' ability to recruit and retain bilingual teachers from the local community and encouraging bilingual high school students to enter the teaching field. The group also supports alternative certification programs that would assist bilingual career changers, instructional assistants, and immigrants who taught in other countries to become certified and teach in the United States.

Finally, Norouzi said that engaging immigrant families in decision-making must move beyond "tokenism" and advisory roles. Power dynamics need to change so that immigrant families' voices and concerns are heard rather than just asking for feedback on issues chosen by the school district. She adds that real relationships in which decisions are co-created are not easy and take time.

Partnerships with Other Community Based Organizations

In addition to partnering with family leadership initiatives, school districts can partner with other community-based organizations to expand the opportunities that they offer to emergent bilingual and immigrant students and their families. Although there are many different types of organizations that enhance school programs, we focus here on three: a summer program, an art program, and a science program.

Aim High

When schools collaborate with community-based organizations, 1+1 can equal 3, according to Aim High executive director Alec Lee. Community-based organizations frequently have special expertise that can augment what schools do. In 1986, Lee co-founded Aim High, a model summer program, which helps schools address the void in summer learning for immigrant families in the San Francisco Bay area.

Aim High is a nationally recognized tuition-free summer enrichment and academic program that targets economically disadvantaged students. The program was intentionally designed to provide high-quality summer experiences for students who were often overlooked and forgotten at an important transition point in their school careers—middle school. Aim High currently serves over 2,300 middle school students each summer, 70–80 percent of whom will be the first in their family to attend college and are primarily of Chinese or Latin American ethnicity.

Students attend Aim High for four consecutive summers beginning with the summer before 6th grade (entering middle school) through the summer before ninth grade (entering high school). The program lasts for five weeks and provides students with academic and enrichment experiences designed to help them set goals for high school and college. The morning portion of the program is focused on academics while the afternoon provides enrichment activities consisting of sport and music electives, field trips, and college visits.

The program has been purposely designed to incorporate small class sizes, culturally relevant curriculum, project-based learning, college and career awareness, and socio-emotional support. A hallmark feature of the program is its youth development course, *Issues and Choices*, which tackles relevant issues from middle schoolers' lives such as peer pressure, bullying, social injustice, racism, and college and career aspirations and equips them with tools to handle these challenges.

Families are encouraged to make a multiyear commitment to Aim High. Upon acceptance to the program, families commit to ensuring students' daily attendance in the summer and to attend family nights. Family sessions are offered in English, Mandarin, and Spanish and include an orientation night, Futures Night, and an end of the summer celebration. The Futures Night is centered around helping students and their families discuss college and career goals after the Aim High program has ended.

When asked about the biggest impact that Aim High has had on its students and families, Mr. Lee shared three key points (personal communication, October 14, 2020): (a) it is a community safe space in which students and families feel honored, appreciated, and their voice is heard; (b) the curriculum is engaging, hands on, and project based; and (c) the program makes a long-term commitment to kids and families for four years. "Kids love it, and families can count on it … it's fun, brings joy and offers a loving community."

SkyART

The Chicago Public Schools were unable to provide art instruction in many schools before they partnered with SkyART in the south and west sides of the city. SkyART, which began in a one-room storefront in 2001 and now occupies more than 6,000 square feet of studios, provides art instruction and therapy for low-income and immigrant students and families in school, at their studios, and virtually.

About half of their participants are Hispanic and all materials and some sessions are bilingual (Spanish and English), including art therapy with licensed therapists in both languages. SkyART, which provides services free to families, believes art is important for everyone but can be particularly empowering for immigrant families who don't normally share their stories. Program Director Devon Van Houten-Maldonado (personal communication, October 27, 2020) said:

> *Art is a wonderful tool for processing trauma and communicating emotions that are difficult to put into words, for children and adults. It can also help families connect through a shared creative activity, perhaps even to escape difficult circumstances if even for a short time.*

During the pandemic, SkyART distributed more than 1,200 art kits that went with webinars and lesson plans created by SkyART teaching artists and staff. Families worked together on the kits at home. SkyART, which was started by an art therapist, also serves hard to reach families by partnering with shelters for domestic abuse and organizations that serve homeless families. They have been instrumental in supplying devices, including iPads and laptops for families who were lacking them.

SkyART defines art broadly to include the culinary arts. One of the family favorites is the Family Table, which helps children grow and cook their own food. Focus group results indicate families are cooking healthier meals at home as a result.

When asked about how other groups could replicate some of their results, VanHouten-Maldonado said that partnerships are important in seeking funding for projects. For example, SkyART and the Chicago Public Schools obtained a Bright Star Community Outreach Foundation grant for an after-school arts program with students and families. Bright Star is a community organization dedicated to community development and advocacy on Chicago's southside. The Chicago Public Schools also have been able to use some of the money earmarked for art teachers because they were not able to fill those positions.

In addition to forming partnerships for funding, VanHouten-Maldonado recommends seeking in-kind services and materials from other organizations. Some people or groups are unable to donate money but can provide services, space, or materials. For example, SkyArt was able to obtain high-quality art supplies through private donations of materials after posting their Amazon wish list on social media and reaching out to art supply companies. Individuals and companies were able to make donations both large and small.

Finally, he says school and community-based organization partnerships are most successful when the organization can offer a service that is different and can reach people who may not otherwise be involved with the schools. VanHouten-Maldonado says ask yourself, "How is my program different and then focus on that."

STEM (Science, Technology, Engineering, and Mathematics)

Many families believe science is too difficult for them, and they may not know whether or how to encourage their children to prepare for STEM (Science, Technology, Engineering, and Mathematics) careers. For this and other reasons, Hispanics are severely underrepresented in STEM fields, which are often the higher-paying jobs and those that offer the greatest future.

CHISPA (CHildren Investigating Science with Parents and Afterschool) was developed to try to overcome the barriers to science for Hispanic families.

CHISPA, which means spark in Spanish, made science accessible to both children and parents.

CHISPA was unusual because it was a broad, complex collaboration, led by the Phillip and Patricia Frost Museum of Science. The collaborative involved 11 science and children's museums across the United States; Padres Comprometidos, a part of UnidosUS, that works primarily with Hispanic parents; and ASPIRA, which provides after-school educational opportunities for Hispanic youth. Both UnidosUS and ASPIRA have local affiliates around the country that were paired with their local museum. CHISPA was funded primarily by the National Science Foundation.

The museums provided science training for staff at affiliates in their local communities so they could pass it on to their participants. The after-school programs used the APEX (Afterschool Program Exploring Science) model, which is a bilingual, hands-on, 32-lesson science program for grades K-5 that was designed by Frost Science in Miami and also funded by the National Science Foundation.

Families who participated in the bilingual Padres Comprometidos con CHISPA program received the standard curriculum (described above in the family initiative section) with the addition of a science component to create experiences, build knowledge, and encourage positive attitudes about science. Families learned how they could do science at home and outside and participated in science experiments with their children. For example, parents and children learned some of the basics of construction. Then, they tried to build a marshmallow and coffee stirrer building that would withstand a simulated earthquake. In another investigation, children and families learned about sound waves and then did experiments to see how sound travels through air, water, and solids.

They also learned what type of preparation is needed to pursue various science careers and how to make sure their children had the appropriate classes before applying for college. In addition, they participated in hands-on science activities at their local museum with their children. Cheryl Juárez, who was principal investigator for CHISPA, says many families visited their local science or children's museums for the first time during the program (personal communication, October 20, 2020).

In order for museums and schools to reach immigrant and minority families, Juárez says, "You can't put an ad for your event in the newspaper and expect people to show up." She believes that building relationships with local leaders of community-based organizations is the best way to involve underserved families.

"You can't just do business as usual. You need to slow down and build relationships first," Juárez said. She calls it the "cafecito" strategy, which involves talking over a cup or two of café with an organization's leaders to get to know each other before asking them to make a commitment or take action. She believes this relationship building is essential to reach new audiences and even to secure funding. Juárez reminds us that "none of this is free," and potential project sponsors or funding organizations like to see that strong collaborations are already in place in order to ensure successful implementation.

Success Stories Key Take-Aways

The success stories reviewed in this chapter vary in their focus, funding, and organization, but they all reflect the ability of schools and families to partner for educational success and improved communities. All of these programs address the needs of their particular contexts, but no one program can meet all needs. Still, there are some commonalities across these programs, and six of them are discussed here.

The successful programs honor all people's culture, language, and values. They view diversity as an asset rather than as a deficit. They build on existing culture, language, and values rather than trying to ignore or erase them. While communities may be divided, the successful programs worked intentionally to bring people from different backgrounds together for common goals.

The programs support capacity building among families and educators. Most educators, including administrators, lack preparation to interact with diverse families, but the successful programs believe in developing those skills among people working in various capacities in the educational system. Families, especially those from other countries, may have difficulty navigating U.S. schools. The programs develop the families' capacity to interact with schools and to advocate for their children.

Shared decision-making is another component of successful programs. Families' roles go beyond volunteering at the school or providing feedback on issues selected by the schools. Schools consider all families as partners in their children's education. Families' expertise is respected, and changes are made based on their needs and concerns.

Successful programs are systematic rather than piecemeal. Although an individual teacher or family can make a difference, successful programs involve broad scale support. Administrators obtain the resources necessary to involve many people over long time periods. They provide the time, support, and money required for sustainable change.

Collaboration is another key component in successful programs. Collaboration takes place among schools, families, community-based organizations, and elected officials. Programs are stronger when they have more supporters and different types of expertise. Districts that are beginning or renewing their efforts to engage emergent bilingual and immigrant families can look for groups in the community that are already working with these families and combine efforts.

Finally, successful family engagement is intentional and well-planned. The authors heard over and over that "it is not easy" and "it takes time." Test scores or graduation rates may not improve in a year, but sustained efforts do pay off for students, teachers, schools, families, and communities.

Activity: Reflection on Successful Practices

Purpose: To reflect on successful practices and improve family engagement, especially for families of ELs and immigrants.

Participants: Individuals interested in family engagement in the schools. This may include school and district staff, families, and community agencies. Interpreters as needed.

Preparation and resources: All of the participants should have an opportunity to read Chapter 10 prior to the discussion.

Description of activity: One way to do this activity is to place participants in groups of four to six with a mix of families, community members, and school staff at each table. Use interpreters as needed. Some of the following questions can serve as discussion starters.

- Have you tried any of the successful practices in this chapter?
- How did they work in your setting?
- What would you like to learn more about?
- Is there something new you would like to try this year?
- How could this idea be adapted to your setting?
- Are there new possibilities for collaboration in your community?

Options: All of the schools and organizations in this chapter have offered to help others interested in improving family engagement. For those interested in more in-depth assistance, some offer paid consulting services.

These discussions could be held in on-line break-out rooms.

Relevant Literature

Dreamers, by Yuyi Morales (2018), is an award-winning book that is an autobiographical account of the author's first experiences coming to the United

States from Mexico with her young son. The book describes the confusion and uncertainty of being in a new country with many new customs. The author describes her liberating experience of finding the local public library and being immersed in the books that she could share with her child. The library became a refuge for her. Immigrant families are often seeking a refuge of familiarity that helps them bridge the distance between their home culture and the culture of school in the United States. *Picture book.*

Just Like Us: The True Story of Four Mexican Girls Coming of Age in America, by Helen Thorpe (2009), is a non-fiction book about the high school and college lives of four young women of Mexican descent who have been close friends since attending a Denver middle school. All graduate from college but two have legal status in the United States and two do not. In addition to describing the personal struggles of the girls, the author discusses their families and the impact of immigration and legal status on their lives. Thorpe, a journalist, places these individual stories in the complex political and legal context of immigration in the United States. *Chapter book.*

Success Stories Websites

Aim High https://www.aimhigh.org/
    CHISPA https://chispanet.org/about
    Klein Independent School District https://kleinisd.net/
    OneAmerica https://weareoneamerica.org/
    Padres Comprometidos https://www.unidosus.org/issues/education/ parent-engagement/
    Parent Institute for Quality Education (PIQE) https://www.piqe.org/
    Portland Empowered https://www.portlandempowered.org/
    Rogers Public Schools https://www.rogersschools.net/
    Shelby County Schools https://www.scsk12.org/
    SkyART https://www.skyart.org/
    Washoe County Schools https://www.washoeschools.net/

References

Allensworth, E. (2013) The use of ninth-grade early warning indicators to improve Chicago schools. *Journal of Education for Students Placed at Risk (JESPAR)*, 18(1), 68–83. https://doi.org/10.1080/10824669.2013.74518

APEX (Afterschool Program Exploring Science). (n.d.) https://www.frost science.org/resource/apex-science-overview-brochure/

Henderson, A. T., Kressley, K. G., & Frankel, S. (2016). *Capturing the ripple effect: Developing a theory of change for evaluating parent leadership initiatives.* Final report, phase 1. Brown University, Annenberg Institute for School Reform. https://www.annenberginstitute.org/publications/capturing-ripple-effect

Mapp, K. L. & Bergman, E. (2019). Dual capacity-building framework for family-school partnerships (Version 2). Retrieved October 19, 2020, from www.dualcapacity.org

Parent Teacher Home Visits. (n.d.). *Building school-family relationships that improve teaching and learning.* http://www.pthvp.org/wp-content/uploads/2016/09/Parent-Teacher-Home-Visiting-Research-Fact-Sheet.pdf

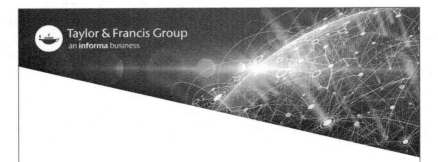

Made in the USA
Coppell, TX
17 January 2022

71775340R00098